J
346
Haskins, James, 1941-
   Your rights, past and present : a
guide for young people / Jim Haskins.
New York : Hawthorn Books, c1975.
   122 p. ; VACAVILLE LIBRARY
   Bibliography: p. 117-118. Includes in-
dex. Discusses aspects of laws dealing
with young people and their right to
work, education, juvenile justice, and
home life.

   1.Children-Law-United States-Juv. lit.
2.Law. 3.Children's rights. I.Title

346'.73'013   KF479.Z9H3
                              74-6665

BOOKS BY JIM HASKINS

YOUR RIGHTS, PAST AND PRESENT

A Guide for Young People

JIM HASKINS

HAWTHORN BOOKS, INC.
PUBLISHERS/*New York*

ACKNOWLEDGMENTS

Grateful acknowledgment is due Carolyn D. Trager, my editor on this book; Mary Ellen Arrington, who typed the manuscript; and Kathy Benson, without whom this book would not have been possible.

YOUR RIGHTS, PAST AND PRESENT

ባ '76

Copyright © 1975 by Jim Haskins. Copyright under International and Pan-American Copyright Conventions. All rights reserved, including the right to reproduce this book or portions thereof in any form, except for the inclusion of brief quotations in a review. All inquiries should be addressed to Hawthorn Books, Inc., 260 Madison Avenue, New York, New York 10016. This book was manufactured in the United States of America and published simultaneously in Canada by Prentice-Hall of Canada, Limited, 1870 Birchmount Road, Scarborough, Ontario.

Library of Congress Catalog Card Number: 74-6665
ISBN: 0-8015-9140-6
1 2 3 4 5 6 7 8 9 10

Contents

1
Why Write About the Rights of Youth?

WHY A BOOK for young people on the rights of youth? Until recently, few publishers would have considered publishing such a book and few young people would have been interested, even if it had been available. Many youths would not have felt they needed to know what rights they had or did not have. Those young people who did need to know did not realize they had any rights, or lack of rights, to find out about. American adults, in general, did not see any need for youth rights. After all, wasn't the American child the luckiest child in the world?

America was then and is still called a youth-oriented culture. A majority of American parents center their lives around their children. The youth market is one of the most important targets for manufacturing as well as advertising. Studies have shown that young people under age twenty-one buy more fast-food (hamburgers, hot dogs, soft drinks, potato chips, candy bars), more records, more cosmetics and more clothing than any other group in the country. Where marketing and advertising are concerned, that's power!

In fact, some adults complain that American youth have too- much power and too much freedom and not enough respect for what they have.

Until very recently, there was not much that young people could say in answer. They knew that there were times when they did not feel so lucky; but they found it hard to explain their feelings. Most did not know that these feelings were shared by other youth as well.

Within the past few years, young Americans have begun to realize that they are not the pampered darlings that they are often accused of being. They have begun to realize that while they might constitute nearly a majority of the national population, when it comes to their rights as persons, they are treated more like a minority group.

In this sense, American youth have much in common with American women. After years of being called the luckiest women in the world, American women are questioning just how lucky they are. They are looking at laws that are supposed to protect them and finding that these laws actually prevent them from enjoying equal rights with men. In the same way, youth are beginning to look at the laws that affect them. Many are surprised to learn just how many rights they do not have.

This is not to say that American youth should belittle the rights they do have, or forget that one hundred years ago young people did not have them, or that even today, in many parts of the world, young people do not have them.

In 1959, the General Assembly of the United Nations unanimously adopted a Declaration of the Rights of the Child. A rather long declaration, its basic provisions were these:

> The child shall enjoy special protection and shall be given opportunities and facilities to enable him to develop in a healthy and normal manner, and in conditions of freedom and dignity; the child shall be entitled from his birth to a name and a nationality; the child shall enjoy the benefits of social security; he shall be entitled to grow and develop in health; the child shall have the right to adequate nutrition; he shall have the right to adequate housing; the child, for the full and harmonious development of his personality, needs love and understanding; he shall grow up in an atmosphere of moral and material security; a child of tender years shall not, save in exceptional circumstances, be separated from his mother; payment of state and other assistance towards the maintenance of children of large families is desirable; the child is entitled to receive education, which shall be free and compulsory; the child shall have full opportunity for play and recreation; the child shall in all circumstances be among the first to receive protection and relief; the child shall not be admitted to employment before an appropriate minimum age; the child shall be protected from practices which may foster religious and any other form of discrimination; he shall be brought up in

an atmosphere of tolerance, friendship, peace and universal brotherhood.

This is a fine declaration, and the rights it sets forth for every child could be enjoyed—in an ideal world. Yet, in many parts of the world today, there are children who do not have even one of these rights. This is not to say that there are cultures in which children are not loved. There has never been a people who did not love their young. The fact is that socioeconomic and political conditions prevent not just the young but people of all ages from enjoying many of these rights.

Such conditions also exist in parts of the United States, but by and large, American youth are fortunate in comparison to their foreign counterparts.

It is necessary at this point to distinguish between two types of rights that are contained in the U.N. declaration: social, or moral, rights and legal rights. Social, or moral, rights are such things as the right to love and understanding, the right to grow up in an atmosphere of moral and material security, the right to be brought up in an atmosphere of peace and universal brotherhood. Legal rights are such things as the right not to be separated from one's mother, the right to free and compulsory education, the right not to be employed before a certain minimum age.

We will be concerned in this book with the legal rights. While the social, or moral, rights are human rights, there is no realistic way to ensure them. Our Constitution states that all are entitled to certain inalienable rights, among them, life, liberty, and the pursuit of happiness, but even the men who wrote those words knew there was no way to ensure these rights to all. By contrast, when the rights contained in the Bill of Rights, such as freedom of speech and freedom of the press, were listed by the Founding Fathers, they fully intended that these rights would be guaranteed to the fullest extent possible by legislation and by the courts.

It is in the area of these legal rights that American youth are so fortunate, although this was not always the case. Unlike the majority of the world youth population, American youth are guaranteed, among other rights:

- The right to a free public education
- The right not to have to work before age fourteen or sixteen; the right not to have to work twelve hours a day, seven days a week
- The right to have their age taken into account in judgment of their crimes or antisocial acts
- Many of the same freedoms of speech and of the press enjoyed by adults
- Many of the same due process, or fairness, guarantees enjoyed by adults

But, while American youth are considerably better off than were young people in this country a century ago and enjoy many more rights than youth in other parts of the world today, there are still a number of rights that young people in this country *do not* enjoy, among others:

- The right to make a will under age eighteen in most

states, which means that, legally, minors' possessions are not their own

- The right to leave school before age sixteen
- The right to leave home until age twenty-one in most states, without parental consent
- The right to the same sentences as adults for acts that are not criminal; indeed, youth can be sent to detention homes for acts that, if committed by adults, would not even be considered crimes
- The right to some of the same freedoms of speech and of the press enjoyed by adults
- The right to some of the same due process guarantees enjoyed by adults

Most young people do not know what rights they do or do not have. A 1974 survey of high school students revealed that 63 percent were unaware of their rights. But this is not a handbook of your rights. A number of such handbooks already exist. What this book does is to put the rights you have into perspective by showing, through an in-depth look at five different areas, how your rights in these areas came about, what rights you still do not have, and, in some cases, what rights you have that can be considered mixed blessings. It's about where you are, where you could have been, and where you still have to go.

2
Youth and Labor

THE FIRST AND one of the most important movements for youth rights in United States history concerned child labor. It was important, first, because it helped spur the establishment of a system of free public education. Second, the struggle to curb child labor can be said to have begun the whole modern American reform movement. Indeed, much of the history of American reform can be written in terms of the movement against child labor. Our nation's child labor laws are truly laws of which we can be proud. Yet, as we will see later, the protection these laws afford youth can also be seen as denying youth's rights.

Once, child labor was a normal part of early life, and it was considered both economically and morally valuable. In colonial times, when America was almost completely agricultural, each family unit was responsible for nearly all the goods it needed. There might have been a local blacksmith who made tools and pots and other metal goods, but food and clothing and furniture had to be made by the family, and the children, from the youngest on up, were expected to do their share. This was so in the towns as well as in more rural areas. Child labor in this sense was generally a good and wholesome thing. It helped keep family ties strong, it provided continuation of craft traditions, and it gave both children and parents a sense of responsibility and accomplishment.

Of course, there were also forms of unwholesome child labor even then. These forms were apprenticeship and public auction of orphans or children from unfit homes.

The system of apprenticeship was brought to America from Europe, where it was an old, respected, and well-regulated operation. Under it, the parents of a boy of twelve or so would apprentice him to an artisan in order to learn a trade. A legal contract was signed, in which the artisan agreed to feed, house, and clothe the youth, to train him in the chosen trade, to oversee his behavior and guard his moral welfare, and usually to teach him to read and write. In return, the youth was to work for the artisan and to obey his commands.

In America, where there was no strong regulation of the apprenticeship system, contracts became increasingly informal, and as the demand for goods grew, the artisan, in need of help, was likely to take on anyone willing to do a job and to treat his apprentices merely as extra hands. There was little time to instruct them in his skill. They learned what they could on their own. He did not pay much attention to their moral welfare. Certainly, he did not want them to drink and carouse late into the night, but that was because they might not feel like working very hard the next day. What the apprenticeship system became in America was a kind of enforced slavery for a youth until age twenty-one.

In colonial times, orphans or children of the poor and incompetent could be auctioned off publicly to artisans or heads of households, for whom they would have to work until age twenty-one. In these situations, there was not even a pretense of a contract. While those who secured the services of these children were expected to treat them humanely and teach them skills, there were no laws or pressures to enforce these expectations.

Still, the number of children who were forced to work under these conditions was small compared to the number who worked with their families at family tasks.

By the early 1800s, this situation was beginning to change. Cities grew, and with their growth it became necessary for the city dwellers to buy goods that they would have made themselves had they lived on farms. Mechanical inventions made many goods easier and quicker to produce. The first factories, in the modern sense, developed. While the majority of people continued to live self-sufficiently on farms, and while most shops and businesses were family enterprises, where the children worked right along with the parents, there were children working in the factories, sometimes under extremely cruel conditions.

Attempts were made as early as 1813, almost all by northeastern states, to regulate child labor. Connecticut was the earliest. In 1813, it passed a law providing for the education of working children by the proprietors of manufacturing establishments.

In 1836, Massachusetts provided that children under

fifteen employed in manufacturing should attend school at least three months a year. Rhode Island, Maine, New Hampshire, and Pennsylvania had passed similar laws before 1860.

In 1842, Connecticut and Massachusetts passed laws restricting the employment of young children to ten hours a day in certain manufacturing establishments. Before 1860, New Hampshire, Maine, Rhode Island, Pennsylvania, New Jersey, and Ohio had followed suit.

Around 1850, laws began to be passed prohibiting the employment in manufacturing industries of children under certain ages: Pennsylvania twelve and thirteen years, Rhode Island twelve years, Connecticut nine and ten years, and New Jersey ten years.

Thus, there were grave abuses in the child labor system even prior to the Civil War.

After the Civil War, however, an era of rapid industrialization took place. Small family businesses were replaced by large, impersonal, commercial factories furnished with tireless and soulless machines.

In terms of industrial and technological process, the machines were wonderful things. The machines and the concept of mass production now made it possible for a product consisting of fifty parts, for example, to be made by fifty machines, each manufacturing one part. With these fifty machines, one hundred products could be made in the time it would take a skilled craftsman, who had to make all fifty parts himself, to make one product.

But the machines also took a lot of the satisfaction out of work. People who made products all by themselves, from beginning to end, could be proud of them. A person who operated a machine that made only one of the fifty parts of a product would find pride pretty hard to summon. In England, when a new mechanical weaving loom was introduced toward the end of the seventeenth century, workmen rioted against the new invention. Later, the same machine was burned in Hamburg, Germany, because it was described as "enabling a totally inexperienced boy" to operate the loom "by simply moving a rod backwards and forwards."

As one reformer, John Spargo, wrote in 1906 in *The Bitter Cry of the Children* about the coming of the machine: "It was as though the new mechanical invention had been designed with the express purpose of laying the burden of the world's work upon child shoulders." While this is the kind of overstatement typical of reformers of the time, it contains some truth. Many of the factory machines were indeed so easy to operate that a child could do so. Also, there were any number of menial tasks to be done around the factory—carrying parts and raw materials back and forth, sweeping the floor, carrying water to the workers—that small children could do.

Quite frequently, children were employed because they could do the work of machines or adults at less cost to the manufacturer. This is why they were employed in such large numbers in the textile mills, why boys were employed in the glass factories at night, why children pasted decorations on candy boxes, why they did all the thousands of jobs they did.

In the cities, many children who had once worked at

home now had to work in the factories to help their families make ends meet. Instead of working for loving or concerned parents, they now worked for employers whose only interest was production and cash gain. Instead of helping their families by working side-by-side with them to produce items they could see and understand, children now brought home meager wages, which were a lot harder to relate to than goods and food.

In rural areas, especially in the South, machines also changed the way of life. Eli Whitney's cotton gin made huge cotton farms both possible and profitable. Other agricultural machines made large farms specializing in other crops financially worthwhile. Children were sent out to work on these farms as their own family farms shrank in size or were lost to creditors.

After the Civil War, too, huge waves of immigration took place—people came in large numbers from Ireland, Germany, Italy, and Poland. Most did not have the means to buy land or to travel much farther than the port cities where the boats upon which they had come to America deposited them. Thus, they settled in the eastern cities and found work in the factories, putting their children to work as well in order to make a living. Even with everyone working, they lived in grinding poverty.

The effects of rapid industrialization and immigration on the number of children under age sixteen in the labor force can be seen in the census figures of the period. In 1870, one out of every eight children was employed. By 1900, about 1,750,000 children—or one out of every six—was employed. Sixty percent were agricultural workers. Of the 40 percent who were working in industry, over half were children of immigrant families.

It is hard for most of us, living today, to envision the kind of life these children led. How must it have been, for example, to be a breaker boy in a Pennsylvania coal mine? In the underground tunnels coal was emptied into chutes leading to machines that washed the coal. A breaker boy's job was to straddle the chute and to pick out pieces of slate and other refuse as the coal rushed past. Boys as young as nine and not much older than twelve, straddled those chutes for twelve hours a day, and one could recognize breaker boys after they had worked for a time, for they became bent-backed, like little old men. One could also recognize them as mine workers by their coughs, which would later develop into asthma and consumption.

Twelve hours a day, seven days a week, 365 days a year; no one got Christmas or Thanksgiving off in the mines. The company did supply a meal—a cold potato, to be eaten while astride the chute. A boy had to be quick to pick out the slate pieces from the tumbling coal. Lost fingers and mangled hands were common, and sometimes a breaker boy disappeared into the chute, to be picked out later, smothered and dead.

Other examples of the conditions in which child laborers worked can be found in Spargo's *Bitter Cry of the Children:*

> I know of a room where a dozen or more little children are seated on the floor, surrounded by barrels, and in those barrels is found human hair, matted, tangled, and blood-stained—you can imagine the condition, for

it is not my hair or yours that is cut off in the hour of death.

Louis H. Hine, in an article in *Survey* entitled "Children or Cotton?" reported:

Millie, aged four, was picking eight pounds (of cotton) a day when I saw her, and Mellie, her sister, five years old, thirty pounds a day. Ruby, a seven-year-old girl on another farm stopped picking long enough to say, as I stood by her, "I works from sun-up to sun-down, an' picks thirty-five pounds a day." I did not see any of the champion child pickers with records of two hundred and three hundred pounds a day, whose achievements are so often recorded in the daily papers . . . . But when we think how many light and feathery bolls little hands must pick to turn the scale at thirty pounds, these common daily averages are sufficiently appalling!

Jacob Riis, the great turn-of-the-century chronicler of the poor in New York City, told of visiting sweatshops, mini-factories in private homes and apartments:

In a Hester Street house we found two little girls pulling basting thread. They were both Italians and said that they were nine. In the room in which one of them worked, thirteen men and two women were serving. The child could speak English. She said that she was earning a dollar a week and worked every day from seven in the morning till eight in the evening.

Reformer Jane Addams told of finding a child of five working by night in a South Carolina mill. E. G. Murphy photographed children of six and seven working twelve and thirteen hours a day in Alabama mills. The accounts of the cruel conditions of the child labor system go on and on and on.

One might ask, how could the parents allow their children to work under such conditions? The reasons are: (1) parents worked under the same conditions; and (2) families needed the money.

Conditions in many of the industries were so terrible that by the time a man reached his forties he was no longer able to work. He might have lost a limb working in the building trades, or contracted rheumatism as a ditcher or sewer-digger, or gotten consumption as a miner or garment worker. Or he might have become unfit to work after a few years on the railroads; the average working life of a railroad worker was *five years!* With a father unable to work, the young children had to help support the family. A Dr. Annie S. Daniel, interviewing 160 New York families concerning their wages, found that in nearly every instance the children's wages, when there were working children, made up the greater share of the family income. Certainly the parents wished for a better life for their children than they had had, but in most cases they were trapped.

Then, of course, there were those children who had no parents or whose parents were unfit. There were the children in reform schools, who, under a system of contract labor, would be released into the custody of a factory owner or farmer to work for him. The lot of these children was, if possible, even worse than that of other children, for they did not have the option of quitting their jobs. If they complained or did not work very hard, they would be sent back to reform school.

Steps to better these conditions began to be taken in the 1880s, although they were hesitant steps. In 1884, New York outlawed contract labor of reform school children and in 1887 Alabama passed a law limiting children under age fourteen to an eight-hour work day. But contract labor continued in other states, and in 1894 the northern owners of Alabama cotton mills secured the repeal of the 1887 law. American society did not really support the attempts to stop the excesses of the child labor system, just as it did not support the idea of government intervention in industry in general. Despite its knowledge of the long hours, meager pay, no play, and the lack of opportunity to learn, the public clung to the idea that work was good for children, that it made them self-reliant little adults, that their labor had a prideful purpose—to bring bread to the family.

Toward the end of the nineteenth century, this attitude began to change. The early reformers were joined by journalists and social workers and concerned private citizens, and the initially small group grew larger and larger. The idea took hold that the working child, rather than being a self-reliant little adult was actually a victim, deprived of his natural rights to play and education.

In 1903 New York State required working children to have certificates attesting to their legal age; children under age fourteen were not to work during school hours. In 1904 a National Child Labor Committee was founded, and in

1907 Congress authorized an investigation of child and female labor.

Progress was slow at first. In New York State, falsified age certificates were very easy to obtain, and even the youngest child learned to answer automatically, "Fourteen, Sir" or "Fourteen, Ma'am" whenever anyone asked his or her age. In other states, factory and farm owners lied about the number and age of children in their employ. Gradually, however, the children were taken out of the factories.

At the same time, state after state was beginning to enact compulsory education laws. It is no accident that the movement against child labor and the movement for compulsory education went hand in hand. As one reformer put it, "The best child-labor law is a compulsory education law covering forty weeks of the year and requiring the consecutive attendance of all the children to the age of fourteen years." Education laws, however, were not just the result of the anti-child-labor movement.

By the beginning of the twentieth century, great advances had been made in technology. More and better machines were in use, and new machines were being invented every day. The immigrant population was being assimilated into the larger American society, and better, higher paying jobs were opening to them. The general level of national prosperity was increasing. Children were less needed in the labor force.

A proposed constitutional amendment, the Twentieth, was introduced in 1924 and was approved by a vote of 297 to 69 in the House and 61 to 23 in the Senate. It read as follows:

Sec. 1. The Congress shall have power to limit, regulate, and prohibit the labor of persons under eighteen years of age.

Sec. 2. The power of the several States is unimpaired by this article except that the operation of State laws shall be suspended to the extent necessary to give effect to legislation enacted by the Congress.

But powerful opposition to the amendment soon became apparent in many states, and three-quarters of the states had to ratify it. The amendment was called a Communist plot; it was said to deny parental rights, to violate the sanctity of the home, and to place the power of the states in the hands of the federal government. It was also objected to as hampering free enterprise, or business. By 1933 only six states had ratified the amendment, and its proponents had to admit defeat.

Still, the very threat of federal legislation in the form of a constitutional amendment caused most of the states to pass their own laws regulating child labor. Meanwhile, state compulsory education laws were strengthened until, in general, no child worked until age fourteen. During World War II, three-and-a-half million American youth between the ages of fourteen and seventeen were working in factories under far from ideal conditions. But then, corporate profits, under the guise of the war effort, usually took precedence. Not until 1950 did federal regulations specify a minimum age of sixteen for most types of work, except farm work. Meanwhile, sixteen was also established as the age at which a youth could legally quit school.

Today, the very idea that young people should work outside the home before age sixteen is condemned. Yet, a growing number of youth and adults are beginning to question seriously the attitudes of our society toward youth labor.

First, the idea that youth should not work does not seem to apply to *all* youth. The children of migrant farm workers, for example, rarely spend more than a couple of months in one school before moving on—if they enroll in school at all.

Second, and more importantly for many American youth today, in saving children from having to work, we have also denied them the right to work.

Many young people would like to work, and it would be good for them to be able to. A child realizes, at a very young age, that someone who works is useful, makes a difference in the world. Work is serious; work is what adults do. Moreover, work is clear-cut and easier to understand than a lot of other things in a child's world. It is a lot easier to understand, for example, than school. In school, an activity is good or bad depending on how the teacher sees it; and often there is no clear reason for doing something except that someone tells you to do it. Where work is concerned, an activity is good or bad depending on whether it gets the job done. Most importantly, work is something one is paid for. Young people need and want the money they could earn to buy things and to save for the future. In a materialistic society like ours, being without money tends to make one feel like a nobody; for many people, having money gives them a sense of self-respect.

Upper-income and middle-income youth can earn money now in many ways. Usually they receive an allowance based on certain jobs or duties done every week. In the summer, jobs are fairly easy to obtain, whether in a relative's business or elsewhere. Yet, their parents tend to see work for their children merely as good experience, not as an alternative to school. The youths have little or no choice; it is taken for granted that they will finish high school and go on to college.

Those whom the denial of the right to work affects most are poor youth. Unable to work, many steal; many also join street gangs. Most who do steal probably would not do so if they had a chance to earn money legitimately and honorably. As it is, many quit school just as soon as they reach the legal age, and as soon as they find jobs they leave the gangs. It is no accident that the membership of most street gangs falls within the nine to fifteen- or sixteen-year-old range; for it is these youths who are trapped in school and unable to work even if they wanted to.

It can be argued that part-time jobs are available to youth and that it is possible to remain in school and work at the same time. This is not really true. Particularly in urban areas, part-time jobs are very scarce, which is why so many cities are trying to develop programs to provide part-time jobs for needy youth. Often, what part-time work is available in the private sector is quite discriminatory against the workers. Within recent years, fast-food chains have blanketed the country, urban and rural areas alike. One of the proudest claims of these businesses is that they employ young people from the neighborhoods around their stores. These claims, however, ring hollow when the actual conditions of employment are considered.

One major chain, for example, hires students and part-time workers almost exclusively and limits them to three-hour shifts. This allows the company to deny their workers all but minimum fringe benefits. This also allows them to pay only the minimum wage, and there is evidence that they are unhappy even about paying the minimum. In an August 1974 article in *New York* magazine entitled "The Burger That's Eating New York," Mimi Sheraton pointed out: "When the new minimum wage bill was being drafted, President Nixon tried to add a provision exempting part-time student workers from the minimum wage requirement. It became known, unofficially, as the McDonald's Minimum Wage Law. . . . A limited variation did pass and is known as the McDonald Rule."

Even for a youth who has reached age sixteen and can legally quit school, there are a number of jobs that he or she cannot get. Under the federal Fair Labor Standards Act, the following jobs are considered too dangerous for youths under the age of eighteen:

- Acting in night work in all but a few cases
- Coal mining—any job in the mines
- Dangerous exhibitions, such as certain circus acts
- Excavation and certain dangerous jobs in agriculture
- Logging and sawmill activities
- Manufacturing and storing of explosives
- Manufacturing of bricks and tile
- Mining other than coal mining

- Motor vehicle driving
- Operation of bakery machines
- Operation of paper-product machines
- Operation of power-driven saws and shears
- Operation of power-driven hoisting machines
- Operation of power-driven metal-forming machines
- Roofing
- Slaughtering and meatpacking
- Street selling or vending
- Wrecking and demolition

Looking at this list makes one aware that there are an awful lot of things a person under age eighteen cannot do, and this is true even of youth who attend or have attended technical schools where they have been taught to use a variety of dangerous machines.

There are objections to the argument that youth should be allowed the right to work if they want to. One is that it would defeat the purpose of free public schooling. Public schooling was designed to give poor children an equal chance with children of higher income families for a better life. To permit young people to work instead of going to school would doom them to a life of unskilled jobs and no advancement. Also, as more poor youth would leave school than those whose families had higher incomes, a policy advocating youths' right to work would be both elitist and racist.

The answer is, of course, that the public school has never worked the way it is supposed to for the majority of poor and minority youth and that forcing them to stay in school until age sixteen only serves to alienate them further from society and to give them more reason to get into trouble with the law.

Another objection is that granting youth the right to work would bring about a return to the old and terrible nineteenth-century system of child labor. It is highly unlikely that such a return would take place. Modern America is very different from nineteenth-century America. While there are still far too many American families living in extreme poverty, our general standard of living is much higher than the average standard a century ago. Youth today are generally not forced to work at a job—they have a choice, they can shop around. And no young people, no matter how bad their jobs, are forced to work under the conditions that nineteenth-century workers did. Labor unions have ensured better conditions in most industries, and there are relatively few industries in which the workers are not organized. Even in those industries, such as agriculture, where unions are not strong, conditions are not as bad as they were a century ago. And minors are protected and restricted by the same laws on the job as adults. They receive the same minimum wage, time-and-a-half for overtime, and the identical protection with regard to hours as adults. Thus, there is little chance that giving youth the right to work will bring about a return to the cruel conditions of a century ago, and there is a good chance that many youth, given the opportunity to earn money and thus gain a measure of self-respect, will give society and the schools a lot less trouble.

If you believe young people should have the right to

work, you should push for that right, by writing to your legislative representatives in local, state, and national government and by urging eighteen-year-olds to speak for you when they exercise their newly acquired right to vote. While you cannot expect great progress immediately, you might be able to get the age at which a youth can work lowered or get some jobs removed from the list of jobs prohibited under the federal Fair Labor Standards Act. If the voting age was lowered, then perhaps the working age can be lowered, too.

You might, in the meantime, also work toward a change in the laws presently on the books that deny youth responsibility for most ordinary employment contracts. If you are not really serious about being a responsible person, these laws are protective. Under them, you can enter into a contract to perform a certain job for an employer and then, if you decide you don't want to do the job, you can break the contract and decline to work without being held liable for your prospective employer's damages, as would be the case if you were an adult and broke your contract. However, if you want to be treated as an adult, you must accept the responsibilities as well as the privileges.

Finally, having indicated a willingness to accept adult responsibilities, you may also be able to secure a change in the present laws that say that as long as you are a minor the money you earn by yourself, by your own work, does not belong to you—a matter that will be discussed in Chapter 5.

3
Youth and School

AN EDUCATION HAS not always been a legal right for American youth. One hundred years ago it was a privilege, and many parents and children either could not or did not seek that privilege.

The idea of public education, however, has deep roots in American history—as far back as 1770 and before. Between 1770 and 1870, many so-called public schools were begun. They were started by a town, a county, a group of people, or just one person. Each state made its own laws governing public education. The federal government made none, feeling that schooling was the responsibility of each state. The schools, therefore, were very different from one another. There was no uniform age for beginning school, no system of classes or grades, little agreement as to subjects taught, no uniformity of fees charged to parents. In the

South and in rural areas of the North, there were very few schools. Before the Civil War in the 1860s, the southern states did not provide for any kind of public instruction at all.

Even where they could be found, public schools were mostly for the wealthier people. Poor people, farmers, and immigrant factory workers, besides being unable to afford the fees for public schooling, could not see the need for their children to have schooling beyond being taught to read and write.

One reason was financial. Children were expected to contribute to the family's earnings. The children of farmers were given chores at a very young age, and by the time they were teen-agers, they were regular farmhands. The children of nonfarm families were expected to go out to work to add to the family's income.

Another reason was that the parents' hopes for their children were not high. Of course they wanted their children to enjoy better lives than they had. But they did not see school as the path to a better life. The way, in their eyes, was for their children to go out to work as soon as possible and to acquire a better life through experience and saved wages.

Between 1870 and 1900, progress in the area of public education continued at a slow pace. In 1870, Michigan became the first state to make public education free, and gradually other states followed suit. In 1872, a United States Supreme Court decision ensured that public funds should be spent for secondary schools. High schools then began to be built in fairly large numbers. Meanwhile, children still did not *have* to attend school in many states. In 1870 just over half (57 percent) of all the children in the United States between the ages of five and seventeen were attending school at least part of the year. The percentage increased steadily each year, however, and the idea that youth should attend high school helped spur compulsory attendance laws for elementary school. By 1900 more than half the states had passed such laws, providing that youth should attend school until age fourteen.

Compulsory attendance became a nationwide policy in 1918 when Mississippi, the last state to do so, joined in making education compulsory. This did not mean that universal attendance was achieved. Children in rural and farming communities and young factory workers often did not attend in defiance of the laws. Gradually, however, more and more young people who were supposed to be attending school were at school.

The reasons for this trend were outlined in the previous chapter on labor and will be repeated only briefly here. Considerable change occurred in American economic life between 1900 and about 1930. Farming came to occupy second place to industry in the nation's economy. The small family business was replaced by the large manufacturing establishment. The population in general became less self-sufficient; goods formerly made at home were now purchased. Youth were no longer needed in the labor market in the numbers required in former years; and something useful had to be found for them to do.

The world was changing in other ways as well. The professions increased in importance, and they required education. Once a man could become a doctor or a lawyer or an engineer by studying his subject or learning about it from a parent or someone else willing to teach him; now formal schooling was needed. Even outside the professions, it was no longer easy for a young person to be successful without schooling. An organized system of schools would, it was felt, prepare all youth for adult life, make up for inadequacies in home and family life, and give all an equal chance to be successful in adulthood.

It was urged early in the twentieth century that schooling be made compulsory even beyond the age of fourteen. A study in Massachusetts at the time showed that the 25,000 children in the study who did not go on with their education after age fourteen were doomed to unskilled jobs. The years they spent in school before age fourteen were *wasted* if they did not continue their education. Yet, despite such studies, the age-fourteen limit continued in most states well into this century. Today, over 50 per cent of all U.S. school districts have statutes making it mandatory for children to attend school from age seven to age sixteen. In some states, level of education rather than age determines when a youth can cease schooling.

To sum up, schooling was once a privilege reserved only for the children of the well-to-do. While it is still seen as a privilege (free public education has never been called a *right* by the Supreme Court, although this is because the Court maintains that education is the province of the states), at least now it is a privilege guaranteed to all children. Many Americans take pride in the nation's free public schooling and compulsory education laws.

Many other Americans, including a considerable number of young people, disagree. They argue that the state's ability to decide when a youth can go to school, where he or she will go to school, and how long he or she must remain in school is a violation of the youth's most basic rights.

In his book *Escape from Childhood*, John Holt states the problem very well:

> The requirement that a child go to school, for about six hours a day, 180 days a year, for about ten years, whether or not he learns anything there, whether or not he already knows it or could learn it faster or better somewhere else, is such a gross violation of civil liberties that few adults would stand for it. But the child who resists is treated like a criminal.

The truant officer is a familiar figure in the stories written about youth since the last part of the nineteenth century. He is usually depicted as an evil man, although sometimes he is a comic character, outwitted by kids who are playing hooky. But, comical or evil, he is doing his job. And his duties have not changed much since the position of truant officer was first created.

In 1909, New York State passed its first compulsory education law. One of the sections of that law provided for "attendance officers." This is how the law viewed their function:

> The attendance officer may arrest without a warrant any child between seven and sixteen years of age and

who is a truant from instruction upon which he is lawfully required to attend within the city or district of such attendance officer. He shall forthwith deliver the child so arrested to a teacher from whom such child is then a truant, or, in case of habitual and incorrigible truants, shall bring them before a police magistrate for commitment by him to a truant school. . . .

You can be arrested for not going to school. You may be bored in school, feeling you are learning nothing. You may be afraid to go to school because a gang bullies you. You may feel that a teacher has it in for you, and you may be right. But none of these reasons makes any difference unless you and your parents are willing to take the time and trouble and risk of fighting the matter in court.

A college student, at least in the last two of the four years (rules vary among colleges), may cut an unlimited number of classes. Class attendance can have little or nothing to do with grades. Students can often make high grades just by reading about the subjects on their own. If they flunk out, it is an individual problem. The police certainly do not care, and there are no truant officers at college.

An adult who does not show up for work is fired, but no disciplinary action is taken. Adults can work wherever they want, providing businesses are willing to hire them. College students can attend any college that will admit them. Public school students, however, must attend the schools to which they are assigned. Only if they can prove that their school does not offer the courses they need can they attend another.

Compulsory education and the steps school authorities

can take to ensure attendance at school are clearly violations of young people's rights as persons. The number of youths, and even the number of adults, who believe this is growing. For those who do, there are ways to begin the fight for youth rights in the area of compulsory education.

If you enjoy the right to vote, you can use it to let political candidates know how you feel. If you are not old enough to vote you can try to convince people of voting age to support your point of view in their voting choices. If you feel strongly enough, you can bring suit against the laws in the courts. Even one favorable court decision is a breakthrough in any cause. The idea is for someone to take the first step. Other courts will be influenced by the decision.

If you feel strongly that you should not have to attend school, there is the possibility that you can make an arrangement by which you might continue your education out of school, being tutored by a parent or another adult. Your chances of success, however, are small.

If the compulsory education laws in each state are ever changed, do not expect the change to happen during the time the laws apply to you. You can, however, work for change for the sake of your younger sisters and brothers and of those yet unborn. Bear in mind, however, that the thing to fight is the current system of compulsory public schooling—not education, not learning.

STUDENT RIGHTS AT SCHOOL

Within the past few years, students have had considerable success in gaining some rights at school.

Until very recently, students had practically no rights in this area. That was because the school was seen as an institution that acted in the absence of parents. The legal term is *in loco parentis* (in place of parents), and the idea that a school should act as a parent when parents are not around is as old as the idea of *school* itself.

Before the American public school system began, childen who were able to go to school were often sent to boarding schools far away from home. As they were usually very young when they left home—anywhere from seven years old to eight or nine —their parents wanted to make sure that they would be properly taken care of and properly disciplined. The arrangements between the parents and the schools their children attended was called a *contractual* one. The parents agreed to pay for their children's education and to give the schools the right to act in their behalf. In return, the schools agreed to educate the children not only in the usual school subjects but also in manners, morality, and other aspects of behavior. A child could be flogged, made to stand in the corner for hours, sent to bed without supper, or any of many other punishments. And in most cases the parents would not object. They felt that the schools knew best.

When compulsory education laws began to be passed in the states, the idea of *in loco parentis* was continued. Students were told what to do, where to go, when to talk, when to move through the halls, when to eat, etc. If they disobeyed, their punishment could range from sitting in a corner wearing a dunce cap or being rapped on the back of the hand with a ruler, to being flogged, suspended, or expelled.

When free public education began, the prevailing attitude on the part of society was that education was a privilege for the student. It was a privilege that could also be withdrawn if the students did not live up to the conditions that went along with it. Put more bluntly, free public education was a gift to poor children and those who benefited from it had to prove worthy of the gift.

This was a grand experiment, but the very fact that it was an experiment opened the door for a lot of repressive tactics. School administrators did not know how hard or easy it would be to control the children of low-income families, believing them to be untaught and undisciplined. Most school administrators and teachers felt a very stern approach would be necessary and the courts upheld their beliefs. As Richard Gyory put it in his *Fordham Law Review* article "The Constitutional Rights of Public School Pupils":

> The courts tended to accept the authority of the schoolmaster with at least as much deference as was accorded the executive branch of government in time of war. A suggestion that a failure to wear a white armband would impede the learning process, or the sporting of a beard and sideburns would undermine discipline in the school, was accepted not merely as persuasive expert opinion, but as established fact.

But it is not necessary to take a modern writer's word for it. The Supreme Court itself held to this view in the past. In 1907, Justice Oliver Wendell Holmes stated, "Education is one of the purposes for which . . . the police power may be exercised . . . ."

Parents, whose taxes were being used to pay for public schooling for their children, did not object to the treatment of their children. Partly, this was because they believed what they were told by educators, politicians, and reformers—"you are lucky that the state is making it possible for your children to go to school." Partly, it was because they believed in firm discipline for their children and in the ability of the schools to maintain this discipline. And partly, also, uneducated parents looked at the schools and the educated people who worked in them and just figured the schools knew better than they. The *in loco parentis* role of the public school system went virtually unchallenged for about eighty-five or ninety years.

People began to question the power of the schools over their students after the civil rights movement became strong, after the historic Supreme Court decision in *Brown* v. *Board of Education, Topeka*, which ruled that separate but equal schools for blacks and whites were unconstitutional, and the various other decisions that resulted from it.

Most Americans, when they think of civil rights, automatically think of rights for racial minorities. But civil rights are available to and due all people, for they are guaranteed under the Constitution. Influenced by the drive by black people for their rights, other people began to fight for rights that they felt were due them. The early attempts by students to exercise protected constitutional rights were found chiefly at the college level. Since about 1969, the primary forum has been the high school. Still, one of the most important early cases involved the elementary school level.

The case concerned religion and the feeling of some parents that their children should not have to pray in school if they did not believe in God or if the prayer they had to say was not of their religion. The case began in local courts and was taken all the way up to the United States Supreme Court. The suit was brought by parents, not by children. The Court ruled in the parents' favor, basing its decision primarily on the constitutional separation between church and state.

Even though the suit was brought by parents and the Supreme Court's decision was based on the separation of church and state, the case opened up a wide range of possibilities for students themselves to fight, in the courts if necessary, for rights they felt they should enjoy at school.

It should be noted here that the fight for student rights has taken place primarily in the public schools. Some changes have occurred in the private schools—the relaxation of hair and dress regulations in some, for example. In the main, however, private schools, by their very nature, are not a forum for the fight for youth rights. Parents who send their children to private schools and, to some extent, the children themselves know and accept the rules of the schools before getting involved with them. If they find they do not like the schools' rules, parents can take their children out of them. Parents of students in the public schools cannot take their children out until the children are sixteen or unless they move to another town or another part of town. Their children must stay and fight for their rights. Since the late 1960s, public school students have been fairly successful in gaining greater rights in several areas.

One such area is that of hair and dress regulations. Let it be stated immediately that the courts do not see hair and dress regulations as very important issues, and indeed they are not very important compared to freedom of speech and freedom of the press. Yet, they are important in the broader sense of student rights in general.

Hair and dress regulations vary from state to state and from school district to school district. In general, however, they are much less strict now than they were in the middle 1960s. Partly, this is because students have considered the issue important enough to fight for change. In the majority of cases, court suits were not necessary; change was brought about through an agreement between students and school officials.

Hair styles and dress styles are fads. In 1965, long hair for guys and pants for girls were just coming into popularity. By 1968 or 1969, many schools were allowing both. It can be said that the change would have occurred without any trouble if the students had just waited. After all, fathers, male teachers, and school principals wearing sideburns and mothers, female teachers, and school principals wearing pants could hardly deny the same rights to students. But there were many students who did not want to wait, who wanted the regulations changed while they were still in school and able to enjoy the new freedoms. While, as has been mentioned above, court cases were usually not necessary, when they were necessary the students were often successful.

The two most successful ways to fight hair and dress regulations were (1) showing that the wording of such regulations was so vague as to be invalid; and (2) showing that school authorities could not prove more relaxed regulations would affect either education or discipline at the school.

Many regulations were very vague. A rule about hair length for boys, for example, could ban extreme haircuts. Students argued, and rightly so, that what one person considered extreme another would not. If the definition of extreme could be decided by the principal or the superintendent of schools, based on his or her personal preferences, then the rule was not valid.

In one case, a high school student used this argument to challenge his suspension from school. The school handbook stated that "extremes of hair style are not acceptable" and the vice principal, deciding that the student's hairstyle was "extreme," had suspended him. The student was never told exactly what made a hairstyle extreme nor was he told how much of a haircut would make his style acceptable. The court found that the regulation was unconstitutionally vague and the student was ordered reinstated.

Some schools had very detailed regulations, specifying the allowable length of a boy's hair or how many inches above the knee a girl's skirt could be or banning pants of any kind for girls. These rules could not be challenged for vagueness. But the reasons for these rules could be challenged. School administrators were challenged to offer proof that a boy with hair down over his ears would learn less than one with shorter hair, or that more rowdy behavior would result if girls were allowed to wear pants.

The following cases show that courts differed greatly, especially when suits of this sort were first brought, as to whether or not relaxed appearance standards created problems in the schools.

In one case, three members of a rock 'n' roll group, who were required by a contract to have "Beatle" haircuts, were denied admission to the local high school. The students took the case to federal court, arguing that their long hair was a form of expression, in many ways like thought and speech, and that their constitutional rights were being violated. The school authorities, however, testified that students with long hair caused problems in the classroom. Their arguments convinced the court, and the decision of the principal not to admit the students was upheld.

In another case, two senior high school students were expelled for wearing long hair styles and disobeying a board of education rule against long hair, sideburns, and beards. The boys took the case to court and argued that they were being denied a freedom due them under the Constitution. While the board of education argued that the students had been a distraction in the classroom and that long hair had an adverse effect on academic performance, the court, in this case, ruled in favor of the students. In finding no solid basis for the regulation, the court observed that there was no direct testimony that the students actually caused any upset in the classroom, nor any evidence that boys with long hair made poorer grades than boys with short hair.

As time went on, in fewer and fewer cases were the school officials able to offer convincing proof that the old hair and dress regulations really made a difference in the quality of education or level of discipline that was maintained in the schools. Meanwhile, long hair, pants, and other styles that once caused great controversy are no longer unusual and are thus not seen as distracting even to those who do not choose to adopt the styles. The issue, therefore, has basically resolved itself.

Today, in most public schools in most parts of the country, hair and dress regulations are minimal. Students may not show up in bathing suits, and it is not likely that they would be successful in a fight for the right to wear bathing suits to school. But public school dress regulations now conform generally to public dress regulations for the rest of society, and that was the students' chief goal in the first place.

Freedom of speech is a much more important issue, and one that federal courts have considered serious enough to become involved in. The freedom-of-speech issue began on the college level in the early 1960s, specifically at the University of California at Berkeley. Students there challenged the long held notion that school officials had the final decision on what could or could not be printed in student newspapers and magazines and on what could or could not be said in student speeches. The students argued that such power on the part of school officials violated their rights to freedom of speech and the press as set forth in the First Amendment.

Many of the students at Berkeley were expelled for their part in the free-speech movement, but the movement led to a revolution on college campuses in the areas of freedom of speech and the press. Today, on most college and university campuses, students are pretty much free to say or print whatever they want. The exceptions involve racial epithets and writings, whether nonpolitical or political, as in the case of pro-nazism that emphasizes anti-Semitism above other aspects of nazism. Administrations retain the right to judge what is truly disruptive, and the courts will deny or uphold this right in individual cases.

The question of the rights of high school students in these areas has naturally followed. So far, however, the situation in the high schools is quite unclear.

Freedom of speech is kind of a catchall phrase that is summoned to justify a variety of actions. It can cover actions that do not involve speech at all, actions that involve actual, oral speech, and actions that involve the written word.

As has been seen, different courts can hand down very different opinions about similar situations. While the opinions of these courts will be cited in future cases, they are not at all binding, although they are precedents (examples that are used in future court cases to justify an argument). A Supreme Court decision, on the other hand, is binding. If you really want a question decided one way or the other, the place to go to is the Supreme Court. Of course, the question must be of a serious enough nature for the Court to agree to consider it. No suit concerning hair or dress regulations was ever accepted for consideration by the Supreme Court. The right of a group of children to wear black armbands in protest against United States involvement in the war in Vietnam *was* considered serious enough by the Supreme Court. Decided in 1969, the case of *Tinker* v. *Des Moines Independent Community School District* proved to be a landmark case, one that would serve as a guide to both federal and state courts for some time to come.

The Tinkers were an Iowa family who held deep beliefs about American participation in the war in Vietnam. Late in 1965, they decided to express their beliefs by wearing black armbands during the Christmas season. The Tinker children attended public schools in Des Moines, and when school officials learned that a group of adults and their children planned to wear black armbands, they adopted a regulation prohibiting the wearing of any armbands in the schools. When the Tinker children refused to obey the regulation, they were suspended.

The children were readmitted to the schools after the planned period of protest was over. But they felt that their constitutional rights under the First Amendment, specifically, their freedom of speech, had been violated. They brought suit in federal district court in 1966. The court, however, ruled that the action of the Des Moines public schools was reasonable in order to prevent disturbance of school discipline.

Not willing to give up, the Tinkers took their case to the U.S. Court of Appeals in 1967, but this court upheld the decision of the lower court. In each case, though, the courts had been divided, with a ruling in favor of the schools passed by a slim majority. This division gave the Tinkers hope, and in 1968 they took their case all the way to the United States Supreme Court.

The judges on the highest court in the land were divided, too; the decision was handed down by a 5–4 majority. But this time, the ruling was in favor of the Tinkers. The Court ruled that the issue did fall into the area of free speech and held that the wearing of black armbands to symbolize a political grievance was close to "pure speech." The opinion stressed the facts of the case, noting that there was no evidence that the wearing of armbands meant any danger or disruption to the school system. It also noted that, while political buttons and other symbols were permitted to be worn, the school picked out a particular symbol to prohibit, and that this was wrong. Thus, based on the facts of the case, the Court ruled in the Tinkers' favor. But the Court went beyond a mere ruling on a single case. The following paragraph is one of the reasons why the Tinker case is considered a landmark case and why it has been cited in many other court cases that have nothing to do with either black armbands or the war in Vietnam. It spoke of the general rights of students:

> School officials do not possess absolute authority over their students. *Students in school as well as out of school are persons under our Constitution.* They are possessed of fundamental rights which the State must respect, just as they themselves must respect their obligations to the State. In our system, students may not be regarded as closed-circuit recipients of only that which the State chooses to communicate. They may not be confined to the expression of those sentiments that are officially approved. In the absence of a

specific showing of constitutionally valid reasons to regulate their speech, students are entitled to freedom of expression of their views.

Freedom of speech when it involves obscene language, either spoken or printed, is another matter. The courts, from the Supreme Court down, do not want to rule on what is obscene and what is not. As the judge in the following case put it, "That area of the law today is about as well-defined as the course of a tornado." An eleventh-grade student in Van Buren, Michigan, was expelled for violating a school regulation against the possession of obscene materials. The principal felt the material was obscene because of the presence of certain words.

The student took his case to federal court on two counts: (1) that his right to freedom of speech had been violated; and (2) that in being expelled without a hearing, he had been denied due process, which, in this case, means simply fairness. The student charged that denying his right to a hearing was unfair.

In the end, the court ruled only on the due process charge. It directed that the school board hold a hearing on the question of expulsion. During the hearing, the student's lawyer showed that the objectionable words were also found in a novel that was required reading for the student and in a magazine that was in the school library. Seeing this evidence, the judge stated that for the school to expel the student for possession of material no worse than the school's own reading materials was "preposterous."

The issue of freedom of the press is more clear, although resolution of the issue has been slow in coming for students below the college level. In a series of decisions in the late 1960s involving college and university publications, several courts around the country ruled that administrators could not legally censor the contents of student publications and could not bar them in advance from appearing. Although several cases dealing with high school newspapers were considered by the courts during these years, not until 1970 did court decisions on such cases begin to show any marked trend toward establishing student rights in this area. Prior to that time, the courts had generally upheld the traditional view that school officials had the last word in deciding what could or could not be printed in student publications.

In July of 1970, a federal district court in Connecticut held that students may publish independent and unofficial newspapers without having the contents screened first by school officials. At about the same time, a New York City Board of Education resolution was passed stating that student judgment would prevail over that of faculty in the editing of *official* school publications. Since that time, more decisions have been made in favor of high school student publications than against them.

There are, of course, two different kinds of student publications, and the distinction has to be made. There are official school publications and *unofficial* publications.

In the area of official school publications, the school has a definite interest in the contents of these publications. In the first place, such a publication reflects the school. Outside readers feel, rightly, that the paper or magazine is expressing the beliefs and opinions of the school. Thus, the school administrators want some control over what goes into those publications. There is also the problem of libel—the printing of damaging and untrue statements. As the editors of official school publications are minors, there is the question as to whether or not they can be sued. The administrators, then, would be the most likely targets for suits. In general, the courts recognize this interest on the part of the schools. But the schools must prove to the courts that libel is involved or that certain articles would actually be damaging to the school's ability to function. In the majority of cases that have come before the courts, the schools have been unable to prove such charges.

Unofficial publications, or independent student publications, are different. If they are produced away from the school, then the school authorities cannot be held responsible for their content. However, the school frequently finds out about them and, if they are distributed on school grounds and are considered disruptive, seizes as many copies as it can and takes action against the student or students involved.

A case in North Dakota shows the change in the courts' thinking from the late 1960s to the early 1970s. In 1967, two seventeen-year-old students passed out a mimeographed "literary journal" to other students and faculty members. The paper included an editorial that criticized the administration's communications with students, claiming that the purpose of the student paper was to improve communication between *parents* and administration. Then followed this sentence: "I urge all students in the future to either refuse to accept or destroy upon acceptance all propaganda that Central's administration publishes. . . ."

The school reacted by taking strong measures against the two students. Three days after the publication was passed out, the students were barred from taking final examinations for the fall term. Two days later they were taken off the debating team. Several days later they were told that their expulsion for the spring term had been recommended. All this took place without any sort of hearing!

Later, a hearing was held, at which the board expelled the students for "inappropriate and indecent language."

The students took the case to federal district court, but the court upheld the school's actions, saying they were appropriate "where speech takes the form of immediate incitement to disregard of legitimate administration regulations necessary to orderly maintenance of a public high school system . . . ."

This decision came before the Supreme Court *Tinker* decision, which, as we have said before, proved to be a landmark case in the area of student rights under the First Amendment. The students appealed the lower court's decision to the U.S. Court of Appeals, and its decision, handed down in 1971, reflected the thinking of the Supreme Court in the *Tinker* case.

The lower court and thus the school were overruled. While the sentence in the publication urging students to destroy or to refuse to accept publications of the high school administration may have crossed the line of acceptable statements, it barely did so. It seemed to have been aimed at getting the attention of the administration more than at inciting the students, and it certainly would have been possible to respond to the editors directly or in writing. The court seemed to favor acceptance of student criticism as a worthwhile influence in school administration. The court concluded that the school officials failed to show that any danger had resulted from the two students' activities.

Above all, the court seemed to be looking to the *Tinker* decision in feeling that the penalty did not fit the crime. A warning to the students would have met the situation better than the actions that were taken.

Racial and religious epithets, obscene language, and articles that actually do create disturbances in schools are still not likely ever to be allowed, and students who distribute these kinds of publications are not likely to get much satisfaction from school or court. However, these students, just like the two students in North Dakota and the Tinker children, are entitled to due process. If the schools overreact to these activities, meting out punishments that are much more severe than the offenses, they will quite often be answerable to the courts.

The idea of due process for school students developed from the idea of due process for youth in general. The *Tinker* decision came not long after those cases in 1966 and 1967 that extended judicial protection to minors, and it is expected by people in the legal profession that eventually the due process aspect of the case will be the area of its greatest effect. As stated earlier, the basic meaning of due process is fairness.

Prior to the 1960s, school administrators had great power

over the lives of their students. Since then, a number of court cases have dealt with the right of students to due process. Two have already been discussed—the *Tinker* case, in which children were suspended for wearing black arm-bands to school, and the case in which the two high school students in North Dakota were overpunished for distribut-ing literature their school found unacceptable. Two other cases of a generally similar nature indicate the criteria on which students' rights decisions are based. In one a high school senior was held to have the right to a lawyer in order to face a charge of cheating where the con-sequences would have been the denial of a state diploma and of certain scholarship and qualifying exam privileges.

In another case, a student who had been suspended for misconduct was held not to have the right to the presence of a lawyer at a guidance conference held to decide whether he should be allowed to return to the school or be trans-ferred to another school.

Other court decisions established precedents for insisting that schools accord their students due process. Making the punishment fit the crime and providing clearly written and definite rules have already been discussed. In addition, some courts ruled that where a charge against a student is serious enough to affect his or her future education or job opportunities, the school must hold a hearing and it must give the student enough advance notice to prepare for the hearing.

Still, while many courts were recognizing students' rights in making such rulings, other courts were ruling against students in very similar cases. Only a Supreme Court ruling can establish a procedure for dealing with particular kinds of cases nationwide, and early in 1975 such a ruling came.

The case the Court had agreed to hear, *Goss* v. *Lopez*, involved nine students who were suspended from Columbus, Ohio, high schools in 1971 during student unrest and racial demonstrations. In Federal District Court the students then challenged the state law that permitted such suspensions for up to ten days without any hearing.

The students argued that this law deprived them of both property (their right to an education) and liberty (by damaging their school records without proof) without due process. The district court panel agreed with the students, and the school authorities appealed directly to the Supreme Court.

The Court, in a vote of 5–4, ruled against the school officials and in favor of the students. "Young people do not shed their rights at the schoolhouse door," read the majority opinion, which set forth certain steps that school officials must take when they suspend pupils for ten days or less:

• The pupil must be given oral or written notice of the charges against him or her.
• If the pupil denies the charges, "an explanation of the evidence" must be furnished against him or her.
• The pupil must be given "an opportunity to present his or her side of the story."

While the Court stopped short of ruling that pupils suspended for short periods had the right to hire a lawyer, cross-examine witnesses for the school authorities or call

witnesses in their own defense, it left open the possibilities
of granting these rights in some future ruling and of ruling
on the question of suspensions for longer than ten days:
"Longer suspensions or expulsions for the rest of the school
term, or permanently, may require more formal procedures."

Only once before, in the *Tinker* case, had the Court
enforced high school students' constitutional rights. This
second decision opened up the possibility of many more
court cases involving students' rights. Some observers
predicted that the *Goss* v. *Lopez* case would revolutionize
school discipline. The Supreme Court justices who had
voted against the Columbus students predicted that the
Court had ventured into a "new thicket" in which they
would continually be asked to rule on questions concerning
whether or not elementary and high school students have
the same rights as college students and adults. Quite
possibly, they are correct.

As to the questions not ruled upon, at least as yet, by the
Supreme Court, various lower courts have established some
guidelines for schools which the majority of schools
probably have followed, if not out of a genuine interest in
and concern for their students, then as a means of
protection from court suits. Then, too, school administrators want to retain control of their own schools,
and the courts certainly want them to do so.

As one judge said, "Law and order in the classroom
should be the responsibility of our respective educational
systems. The courts should not usurp this function and turn
disciplinary problems, involving suspension into criminal
adversary proceedings, which they definitely are not."

Another judge put it: "It is to everyone's advantage that decisions with respect to the operation of local schools be made by local officials. The greater the generosity of the Board [of Education] in fostering, not merely tolerating, students' free exercise of their constitutional rights, the less likely it will be that local officials will find their rulings subjected to unwieldy constitutional litigation."

This attitude means that there is a great opportunity for students to bring about change within the schools without having to resort to the time and expense of court suits. If students will inform themselves of the rights granted to them by the courts and the rights suggested by the courts, they can move to ensure that those rights will be theirs. While it can hardly be said that the idea of the school's acting *in loco parentis* is dying, it is evident that there is now a greater burden upon the school authorities to show justifiable reason for exercising disciplinary control over students when their constitutional rights are involved.

The issue of students' rights had become a very important one by the mid-1970s, so important that even the United States Congress had become involved in it. This involvement concerned student records.

The keeping of records on individual students has always been an important part of the educational bureaucracy. Student records can include everything from health profiles to grades to attendance figures to notes on behavior made by teachers and school authorities. These records have considerable effect upon the students' futures, both the following year and the rest of their lives.

How does a student's record affect the student? It can decide how a new teacher views the student. Many educators seeking to reform the educational system criticize the easy access teachers have to their students' records. Too many students entering a new grade and a new classroom begin with a handicap. Their teachers have read their records from previous grades and classes and have already formed opinions without trying to get to know the students' behavior and abilities themselves. Thus, a student who may have been unruly in his or her fifth-grade class is seen immediately as a behavior problem by the sixth-grade teacher.

Should this student wish to apply to college six years later, his or her record, containing whatever references to unruly behavior teachers felt like placing on the record, goes to the college. It could make the difference between acceptance and rejection by the college.

The police, too, had access to these records, as did other law-enforcement agencies; and they were able to look at them for any reason whatever. In 1973, a fifteen-year-old high school student in New Jersey wrote to the headquarters of the Socialist Workers Party in the course of research for a social studies project on political ideologies. She did not know that the FBI had ordered the screening of all mail sent to or by the allegedly subversive organization. She also did not know that, because of that letter, a file had been started on her by the FBI. She found out about it all when an agent visited her school to check on her record! The student brought suit against the FBI for the destruction of the file and won, but what if the agent had been able to check her school record without her finding out? What if her record had shown that she had participated in an antiwar demonstration or worn a political button? The court did not address that question.

In the past neither students nor their parents have been allowed to see student records. Thus, they had no way of knowing what was on them, unless they were informed by school authorities. They had no way to find out whether or not Johnny's sixth-grade teacher, who showed a distinct dislike for Johnny, wrote anything negative into his record. Even if they did find out, there was little they could do about it.

The courts tended to uphold the schools' right to keep records, to decide what should and should not go on a student's record, and to withhold these records from students and parents. In 1969, a judge in Pennsylvania denied a suit brought by twelve minors who wanted to keep school officials from placing on their school records notations that they had distributed literature or worn armbands bearing the words *HUMANIZE EDUCATION* at the graduation ceremonies. The district court noted that, under the *Tinker* decision, passing out the literature and wearing the armband were constitutionally protected rights. It also stated, however, that "school officials have the right and . . . a duty to record and to communicate true factual information about their students to institutions of higher learning, for the purpose of giving the latter an accurate and complete picture of applicants for admission." These were arbitrarily chosen bits of information, and one wonders what the duty was to record such selective information out of the thousands of details that might be noted on the student's records.

There were some court cases in which a suit to remove information was successful. Usually, these involved instances where the student could prove school officials wrong. In 1967 and 1971, New York courts, after finding a grooming regulation unconstitutionally vague, directed that the notation on the student's record that he had violated the regulation be removed. A Connecticut court did the same thing in 1970. However, the schools in these cases might well have gotten around the ruling by noting, not that the students had violated grooming regulations, but that they were poorly groomed.

On New Year's Eve, 1974, however, a major breakthrough came in the area of student rights regarding their records. President Gerald Ford signed into law an amendment to the Education Act Amendments of 1974, known as the Buckley Education Amendment because it had been sponsored by Republican Senator James L. Buckley of New York.

The law went quite far in establishing legal protection of students' rights with regard to who had access to their records and what goes into those records. Basically, the law's provisions are these:

• Records of students on all educational levels are no longer closed to students and their parents. Up to the age of eighteen, while students themselves cannot have access to their records, their parents can; after age eighteen, *only* students have access to their records.

• If students or their parents find what they consider damaging and unproved material in their records, they may petition to remove it. And the school must establish hearing procedures to deal with the matter. Whether or not the petition is successful, the fact that a challenge has been made will also go into the record.

• Department of Health, Education and Welfare guidelines on the amendment state that for schools to remove damaging material from students' files would "subvert" the intention of the amendment, but there is no provision in the amendment specifically prohibiting such action by the schools. The reason, of course, is that school removal of damaging material from students' files will usually only benefit the students.

• No longer are student records open to the police or the FBI or prospective employers without *written permission* from the student or the parent of a student under eighteen. The only cases where this written permission is not required involve the normal and necessary transferral of these records from school to school in case a student changes schools or from high school to college or university.

In sum, the amendment does much to right the wrongs that have been done to students in the area of student records. Still, young people should not now become complacent about their records. The whole question of records is something you ought to be aware of. The older you get, the more records will be kept on you by someone, somewhere. Recently, adults have begun to complain about this invasion of privacy. It is good that something has been done to halt that invasion where it first begins to be serious.

Though there have been many important gains in student rights at school, there is still much to be done. Corporal punishment is one such area. Traditionally, any teacher could punish a student bodily, by flogging, rapping on the back of the hand with a ruler, shaking, pushing, etc. Unfortunately, some teachers, probably a small minority, used corporal punishment excessively and not only as disciplinary action but to take out their own unhappiness on their students. Such excesses led to court suits brought by parents to ban corporal punishment in the schools, and many states passed laws making such punishment unlawful. Where such laws do not exist, the law regards corporal punishment as something a teacher may inflict to a reasonable degree to maintain discipline and to compel compliance with reasonable rules and regulations. A teacher is not justified in using corporal punishment to enforce an unreasonable rule, to compel pupils to pursue study forbidden by their parents, or to compel them to do things that their parents have requested they be excused from doing. The law goes on to say that the teacher should use discretion in administering corporal punishment and that the punishment should not be "cruel or excessive, or wanton or malicious." However, the law concludes by saying, "punishment is not necessarily excessive because the pupil suffers pain or bruises."

It is just this kind of statement that allows abuse of students by a small minority of teachers. Some students, by their behavior, invite a slap or a shake. But putting the student in a position in which he or she can become a victim is a violation of that student's constitutional rights.

Below is a list of some other rights that public school students, in general, do not enjoy at present.

- You do not have the right to attend a school other than the one to which you have been assigned.
- If you are pregnant and unmarried, you may not attend school until your pregnancy is over. If you are pregnant and married, you may or may not be allowed to attend school, depending on the local school board.
- You do not, generally, have the right to privacy with respect to your locker, desk, etc. Schools may search them.
- You may not belong to a secret organization.

Just how many rights a student enjoys depends upon the particular school and the part of the country in which it is located. There are no national laws governing education in this country, and there is nothing in the Constitution about the rights of school pupils. Thus, many questions must be answered case by case, and regulations will evolve in this manner. The courts, quite plainly, do not want to assume the responsibility of deciding on everyday school affairs. Still, the fact that the courts have heard a number of cases and decided for the students has brought constitutional considerations into everyday school affairs. Knowing this, school administrators are now less likely to use their power arbitrarily or carelessly.

The future, then, is hopeful, for with the Supreme Court decision in the *Tinker* case and the increasing recognition of students' constitutional rights in everyday school activities, there does not appear to be any logical basis for limiting those constitutional rights to a particular area.

4
Youth and Juvenile Justice

ONE HUNDRED YEARS ago, if you had committed a crime, you would have been tried in the same courts and sentenced to the same prisons as adults. And if you had committed a crime punishable by death, no matter how old you were, you could very well have been sentenced to death. As late as the beginning of this century, an eight-year-old was executed for arson and a thirteen-year-old for murder.

Of course, conditions for young offenders differed from state to state and from city to city. In the 1850s Ohio and Massachusetts decided that young offenders should receive more humane treatment and instituted farm reform schools for youthful offenders. The philosophy behind these schools was a sound one—through the hard, honest work of the farm, a youngster would gain self-respect. Other states followed suit. After the Civil War, however, welfare services of the individual states expanded greatly and less money was earmarked for the reform schools, which were thus forced to earn part of their own expenses. Founding of new farm schools stopped, and some already in existence were converted into nonfarm schools. It became standard practice to contract or hire out the inmates to local manufacturers, who had complete control over the youths during working hours. While it is difficult to know how many manufacturers took unfair advantage of the situation, instances of brutality and exploitation were not uncommon. Generally, there was nothing the youths could do to the manufacturer or his plant, so they retaliated against the schools that hired them out. Rioting, arson, and even murder occurred at nearly every institution.

What made life in one of these reformatories even worse was that sentences were indeterminate. A thirteen-year-old, sentenced for a relatively minor offense, could conceivably remain a virtual prisoner until he or she became an adult under the law. It was a great irony that attempts to improve a system that treated juveniles just like adults resulted in the denial to juveniles of the rights they had enjoyed, with adults, under the old system.

This irony did not go unrecognized, and there were several cases around 1870 in which the idea of *parens patriae*, or the state's right to act in the role of parent, as it was exercised by reform schools, was challenged. Under the guise of a parent, institutions detained their young inmates, even when they were just orphans or vagrants, based on the theory that they were educating them and protecting them rather than punishing them.

The most important of these challenges took place in

Illinois in 1870, in the case of *People* v. *Turner*. In handing down his decision, the judge of the case stated that the reform school boy was really a prisoner, and because he was a prisoner he at least ought to have the same legal rights as an adult convict. Later decisions, however, did not support the judge in *People* v. *Turner*, and little was done about the rights of reform school youth.

Reform schools continued to be considered preferable for youthful offenders to adult jails, and over the years more and more states did separate youths from adults. But adoption of reform schools proceeded at a very uneven rate nationally.

In the deep South provisions were not made for juvenile offenders until after the turn of the century. In Chicago in 1899, 322 boys ranging in age from nine to sixteen years were sentenced to Bridewell, the city prison. All had been convicted of disorderly conduct, a catchall term that included offenses ranging from burglary or assault with a deadly weapon to picking up coal on the railroad tracks or setting bonfires or playing ball in the street. In the prison, they shared cells with hardened criminals. The prison was notorious for its horrible conditions, and it was not uncommon for a judge to pardon a child offender rather than send him there.

It was conditions at Bridewell that caused reform-minded residents of Illinois to push for an entirely new system. It was not enough, they felt, merely to distinguish between adults and minors *after* sentencing. Adults and youths should have entirely separate court procedures, separate sentencing procedures, and separate detention institutions. In 1899, the Illinois Juvenile Court Act established the first separate, noncriminal court for children in the Chicago area who violated the criminal law, or children who had been brought to the attention of the court as neglected, homeless, or "otherwise disreputable."

It must be understood that the juvenile court was not a separate building or even a separate room. It was nothing more than a different set of procedures for dealing with youth, and it became a model for juvenile court systems in other states.

The juvenile court system took delinquent juveniles out of the criminal court and put them into the civil court. The distinction between civil law and criminal law is not always a clear one. Basically, civil cases involve conflicts between individuals. Divorce falls under civil law. If a man runs his car over his neighbor's hedge and refuses to pay the damages, the neighbor takes him to civil court. Criminal cases always involve actions against society and are prosecuted by "the people," as in *The People* v. *Johnson*. Crimes are seen as actions that injure the total society, even though they may be committed only against a single person.

In civil cases, punishment per se does not exist. A fine or payment of damages may be in order, but not actual punishment. In criminal cases, there is punishment, and it can be very extreme, as extreme as the death penalty. The idea behind the juvenile court was that young people were not really responsible for their actions and that those who were not responsible could not be punished.

In the juvenile court there are no trials; there are adjudicatory hearings. An adjudicatory hearing does not end in a verdict of guilt or nonguilt but in an adjudication—a statement of the youth's condition: neglected, delinquent, dependent, in need of supervision, or otherwise. Based on this adjudication, the juvenile court judge would decide that the youth should be returned to his or her family, placed in a foster home, or sent to a youth facility. These possibilities were not considered punishment, but as action taken for the youth's welfare, to provide a home of some sort, instruction, rehabilitation.

The Illinois law was hailed by many as forward-looking and humane, and the juvenile court movement soon spread throughout the country. By the 1920s almost every state had instituted some sort of legal provisions for delinquent and neglected youth.

Before going further, it is important to establish who is a juvenile and who is not; even though we have been talking about the beginning of the juvenile court, it makes sense to give the present-day ages after which one is no longer considered a juvenile. These ages can be changed at any time, and it is always best to check your own state laws if you intend to take action based on a question of age.

Alabama	18	Connecticut	16
Alaska	18	Delaware	18
Arizona	18	District of Columbia	18
Arkansas	21	Florida	18
California	21	Georgia	16
Colorado	16	Hawaii	18
	if the crime is punishable	Idaho	18
	by death	Illinois	17—boys
	18		18—girls
	otherwise		

62

Indiana	16	New Mexico	18
	if the crime is punishable	New York	16
	by death	North Carolina	16
	18		certain crimes punishable by
	otherwise		ten years' imprisonment
Iowa	18	North Dakota	18
Kansas	16	Ohio	18
Kentucky	17—boys	Oklahoma	18
	18—girls	Oregon	18
Louisiana	17	Pennsylvania	18
	with optional jurisdiction	Rhode Island	18
	to 21		but jurisdiction may be
Maine	17		waived
Maryland	16–18	South Dakota	16–18
	depending on county	Tennessee	16–18, generally 17
Massachusetts	17	Utah	18
Michigan	17–19	Vermont	16
Minnesota	18	Virginia	18–21
Mississippi	18	Washington	18
Missouri	17	West Virginia	18
Montana	18	Wisconsin	18
Nebraska	18		but offenders over 16 may be
Nevada	18		transferred to criminal courts
New Hampshire	18	Wyoming	19—boys
New Jersey	16–18		21—girls

As you can see, these ages vary from state to state. In all states, until you have reached your fifteenth birthday, you may not be convicted of any crime except murder in the first degree (willful and planned) or murder in the second degree (unplanned and committed in anger). Between the time when you cease to be a delinquent and the time when you become an adult (this, too, varies from state to state, from as low as seventeen to as high as twenty-one) you may

63

still not be treated as an adult. Usually, you are called a youthful offender rather than an adult offender. You will be tried in a criminal court, but if you are convicted, you are convicted for being a youthful offender, never for a crime, and sentencing is more lenient.

From its beginning the juvenile court system was opposed by those who questioned its constitutionality. The new court was quite definitely a noncriminal court of equity. A court of equity is, by definition, assumed to deal with juvenile cases in the best interests of the child and need not be too concerned with the child's legal rights. Thus, attempts to challenge the constitutionality of the juvenile court—which deprived children of such basic rights as the right to appear with counsel, the right to a jury trial, or the right to remain silent in the face of an accusation of crime—failed.

In a decision reached in the case of *Cinque* v. *Boyd* in 1923, the Connecticut courts held that the juvenile court process was a "civil inquiry, to determine whether, in a greater or lesser degree, some child should be taken under the direct care of the State and its officials to safeguard or foster his or her adolescent life." Given this high ideal, such minor considerations as letting the child know why he or she was being taken away from home were not very important. The Pennsylvania Supreme Court put it this way in *Commonwealth* v. *Fisher:* "The natural parent needs no process to temporarily deprive his child of its liberty . . . to save it and to shield it from the consequences of persistence in a career of waywardness, nor is the State, when compelled, as *parens patriae*, to take the place of father for the same purpose, required to adopt any process as a means of placing its hands upon the child and lead it into one of its courts." So much for the attempts to fight the juvenile court system.

Within the space of a few years, a revolution had occurred in society's idea of the child. Just as, in the case of child labor, children were no longer seen as self-reliant little adults but as victims, so, in the area of criminal justice children were seen not as little adults completely responsible for their acts but as immature beings not wholly responsible for their acts. Those who supported this view sincerely felt that they were doing the most humane thing, and perhaps they were. The trouble is that instead of developing as intended, the juvenile court system became as punitive in its own way as the earlier system. In retrospect, the juvenile court movement was a step backward in many ways, rather than the progressive move its founders believed it was.

For one thing, the new juvenile court considered as offenses acts that, if committed by adults, would not even be considered crimes. Truancy, running away from home, having sexual relations, and drinking alcohol were just some of the actions typically not punishable when engaged in by adults but considered punishable when engaged in by juveniles. In addition, an offense category existed for juveniles for which no similar category existed for adults. Delinquency statutes included a general category of children who were incorrigible. In the words of the Tennessee act, this meant those who were "beyond the control of parents or guardian or other lawful custodian."

For another thing, the lack of formality that was supposed to make the juvenile court more human than a criminal court proved, in the long run, to make it less human. Youths could be brought to court without their parents' even knowing what they were charged with. Police officers, social workers, and other witnesses could say just about whatever they wanted to. Statements like, "Everyone in the neighborhood knew he/she was no good" were admissible as evidence, even though they constituted hearsay evidence. The accepted definition of delinquent behavior was terribly vague and did not involve proof of a pattern of antisocial behavior.

By the 1940s and 1950s, in response to increasing criticism of this lack of due process, juvenile courts began to take some steps toward more formal procedures. They required that the youth and his or her parents be notified of the charges against him or her. They began to make a distinction between direct evidence and hearsay evidence and to be more critical of hearsay evidence. They clarified their interpretation of delinquent behavior. They also gave greater consideration to whether or not the punishment fit the crime, and, occasionally, commitments to institutions were reversed because the evidence did not justify such harsh treatment.

Still, these steps toward greater formality came nowhere near the due process to which adults were entitled in criminal court. Not until the last half of the 1960s would youthful offenders' rights to due process be established.

Although this question was considered by the U.S. Supreme Court in a case in 1966, it was the 1967 *Gault* case that brought about the closest thing yet to a landmark decision in the area of due process for juveniles.

Fifteen-year-old Gerald Gault allegedly made an obscene telephone call. He was taken into custody by the sheriff of Gila County, Arizona, without notice to his parents, and put in detention. Then his mother was called and advised that her son was in detention for making an obscene telephone call and that a hearing would be held the afternoon of the next day in juvenile court.

A petition was filed on the day of the hearing, but it was not served on or shown to the youth or his parents. Nor did it give a specific charge; it merely stated that Gault was a delinquent minor. The person who had made the complaint about the telephone call was not present at the hearing and no one was sworn. The juvenile officer stated that the youth admitted making the lewd remarks. The confession, however, occurred out of the presence of the youth's parents, without a lawyer, and without his being advised of his right to silence. Neither Gerald Gault nor his parents were advised of his right to silence, of his right to be represented by a lawyer, or to have counsel appointed if they could not afford a lawyer.

The juvenile court found Gerald Gault to be a juvenile delinquent and committed him to the Arizona State Industrial School "for the period of his minority," or until age twenty-one. The case had to be taken all the way to the U.S. Supreme Court before the decision was made that perhaps Gerald Gault had been treated unfairly!

To be fair here, it must be stated that, at that time, the right to due process in the courts had not been very long established even for adults, at least in state courts. Although the right of a defendant to due process was recognized in the federal courts in the early decades of this century, the state courts were relatively free to operate as they wished, bound only by their own constitutions and state court interpretations. Federal courts recognized the privilege against self-incrimination, the right to a jury trial, and the right to assigned counsel in major cases before 1930. As to the state courts, the very first right-to-counsel case coming from a state court and decided in favor of the accused by the U.S. Supreme Court occurred in 1932. And it was not until 1966, in the *Miranda* v. *Arizona* decision, that the U.S. Supreme Court ruled that persons must be advised of their rights to counsel and silence.

Thus, while it is hard to excuse juvenile courts for denying due process to young people even into the 1960s, it is understandable in light of the fact that due process was denied even to adults until after 1930. The history of this country shows that recognition of youth rights generally seems to follow recognition of adult rights.

In the *Gault* case, the Supreme Court ruled that the youth had been denied due process and established four rights:

• The right to written notice of the specific charge, to be given to the youth and his or her parents or guardian far enough in advance of the hearing to permit preparation.

• The right to notification of the youth and his or her parents of the youth's right to be represented by counsel, either retained by them or, if they are unable to afford a lawyer, appointed by the court.

• The right against self-incrimination.

• In the absence of a valid confession, the right to have a determination of delinquency and an order of commitment based only on sworn testimony and cross-examination of witnesses.

What it did *not* establish were two other rights for juveniles:

- The right to a jury trial.
- The right to have one's involvement in illegal activity proved by a high standard of proof.

In not establishing these rights, the Supreme Court was being neither conservative, nor reactionary, nor antiyouth. The judges, instead, were mindful of a very important distinction: the difference between civil law and criminal law. Part of the point, way back in 1899, of separating the juvenile court from the criminal court, was to take youthful offenses out of the realm of criminal law and to put them into the realm of civil law. If the Supreme Court were to establish in the juvenile courts all the procedures that were required in the criminal courts, then there would no longer be any difference. And if there were no difference, then there should not be a juvenile court separate from the criminal court.

Still, the question of due process had become very important; and having become important in the case of adult criminals, it eventually became important for juvenile offenders. The issues of trial by jury and high standard of proof are both subjects that are currently being argued in the courts. Individual cases have been decided both ways, but certain trends are evident.

In the area of a high standard of proof, the most important case so far has been the case *In the Matter of Samuel Winship*, decided by the U.S. Supreme Court in

March 1970. Samuel Winship, age twelve, was accused of stealing $112 from a woman's purse. At the hearing, the judge found that the youth was delinquent and ordered him placed in a training school, where he could very well have been forced to stay for six years, or until he was eighteen and had reached his majority. The same crime, if committed by an adult, would have been called larceny, and the period of confinement would have been much, much less. What the youth challenged, however, was not the system that allowed him to be punished far more severely than an adult for the same crime, but the system that allowed a juvenile court judge to decide his guilt or innocence without reliance on the standard of proof beyond a reasonable doubt.

When the Supreme Court heard the case, the hearing judge admitted that his finding of delinquency was based on a preponderance of the evidence, and he rejected the necessity for proof beyond a reasonable doubt. A majority of the Supreme Court judges disagreed, and their finding that Samuel Winship had been denied due process in not being allowed the right to be proven guilty beyond a reasonable doubt was very important for future cases. The judges were still mindful of the difference between the juvenile court and the criminal court, and of not handing down a decision that would erase the distinction. Justice J. Harlan addressed this point directly in his opinion, saying that, while procedural requirements imposed by due process in a criminal case were not automatically the same as those in a juvenile case, the requirement of proof beyond a reasonable doubt in determining delinquency would not endanger the basic reasons for creating juvenile courts in the first place.

Also, by addressing only the question of proof beyond a reasonable doubt and not the broader question of equal protection under the law, the Court did not touch the basic aspects of the juvenile court—its flexibility, its confidentiality, its informality, and the speed of the juvenile process.

In the area of the right to trial by jury, the trend is very definitely against granting this right in juvenile proceedings. The two most important cases so far were decided by the U.S. Supreme Court in 1971.

One case, *McKeiver* v. *Pennsylvania*, involved separate proceedings against two boys, aged fifteen and sixteen, charging acts of juvenile delinquency. The trial judge in each case denied a request for jury trial and found the youth delinquent.

In the other case, *In re Barbara Burrus, et al.*, a group of young people, ranging in age from eleven to fifteen, were charged in Hyde County, North Carolina, with various acts arising out of a series of demonstrations protesting school assignments and a school consolidation plan. The trial judge denied a request for jury trial and, after declaring the youths delinquent and committing them to custody, suspended the commitments and placed each youth on probation.

Both cases went all the way to the U.S. Supreme Court, and in both cases the Court ruled that the due process clause of the Fourteenth Amendment did not assure the right to jury trial in a state juvenile court proceeding.

Few courts have adopted a jury trial requirement. While this means that youth are thus denied a right that is guaranteed adults in criminal court, there are reasons why this right is not as necessary as it might seem. For one thing, as mentioned earlier, trial by jury is one of the few procedures that make the juvenile court different from the criminal court. While the juvenile court, since its beginning, has left much to be desired, it is still a better way to deal with juvenile offenders than a regular criminal court. For another thing, the trial-by-jury system would greatly slow down the juvenile court process. Presently, the American court system moves very slowly, because of all the requirements of due process. While this is not to argue that youth rights should be denied for the sake of expediency, it can be said that juvenile rights are usually best served by speedy but fair judgments. Finally, it may be argued that if all other juvenile court proceedings are fair, and a high standard of proof is required, the safeguard of a jury might not be necessary.

More important for America's youth, now that most of the rights under due process are guaranteed as they are for adults, is what happens before and after the juvenile court judge makes his decision and what kind of behavior is seen as delinquent.

First, there is the matter of what to do with a juvenile between the time he or she is picked up and the time his or her case is heard in juvenile court. A survey done in 1968 of 1,214 juvenile courts across the country revealed that over 31,000 youths picked up by the police and awaiting action on their cases were held in adult jails. In addition, 20,000 were kept in juvenile detention homes. In most instances, if they had been adults, they would have been permitted out on bail. This situation has not improved and something has to be done about it. Until this practice of detainment is prohibited, no youth in America can be sure that if he or she is picked up by the police on a charge of vagrancy or theft or running away or incorrigibility he or she will not be virtually imprisoned, without chance of bail, whether or not he or she is guilty and whether or not the offense committed is a serious one.

Of course, detention after arrest and before trial is not always required. Often, the youth is released in the custody of an adult or sent to a foster home rather than to a children's shelter. But bail is almost never granted in a juvenile case. The one federal case on the subject says only that, before taking a youth out of his or her home, the court has to have a decent detention facility to which to send him or her. Unfortunately, the definition of decent varies greatly from state to state and town to town.

Very serious, too, is the matter of what acts or behavior can result in a youth's being sent to a shelter or school or foster home. Old laws listed truancy, running away, sexual activity, and drinking alcohol as acts that were punishable if done by minors but not if done by adults. Old laws also included the catchall category of incorrigibility, for children beyond the control of their parents or guardian.

Beginning in the early 1960s, new laws have been passed that recognize this inequality, especially in the case of youths formerly dealt with under the incorrigible category.

The California Juvenile Court Act of 1961 and the New York Family Court Act of 1962 both focused on separating runaways, truants, etc., from youths who commit acts that would be punishable if committed by adults. The New York law created the category of "persons in need of supervision" for noncriminal but illegal conduct, and the California law placed such conduct in a different provision of the juvenile court law than that covering criminal acts.

These two acts, however, have not lived up to expectations. New terms are now used, but action has hardly changed. In New York, persons in need of supervision may be committed to the same training schools as delinquents. In California, youths who have committed illegal but noncriminal acts may not be committed directly to the Youth Authority, which runs the California training schools, but may and often do wind up there anyway as probation violators, even though they were placed on probation originally because their acts were not criminal ones.

Despite the laws, in other words, the trend is still toward retaining jurisdiction over noncriminal violators and toward continuing to deal with delinquents and misbehavers in the same institutions. In reality, there is still no real separation between criminal and noncriminal behavior among minors.

This situation can be changed, however, and probably will be eventually. Certain U.S. Supreme Court decisions have pointed the way to this change, although they have not specifically ruled on the matter. The *Gault* decision in 1967, for example, implied that juvenile court jurisdiction over youths who have committed no specific criminal act (Gerald Gault was accused of making an obscene telephone call) and yet face a period of detention would be subject to constitutional challenge on several grounds. The Supreme Court decision in *Robinson* (1962) indicated that the cruel and unusual punishment clause might be held to invalidate juvenile court jurisdiction over incorrigible children. It is likely that the paths pointed to in these decisions will be followed.

Finally, youth rights are still being denied in the area of adequate facilities for juveniles who have been placed in institutions. In many cases, conditions in modern-day detention homes or training schools or children's shelters are not much better than those of a century ago.

In 1974, a scandal erupted over conditions in a children's shelter on Manhattan's East 104th Street, on the edge of East Harlem. The shelter formerly housed young boys aged seven to twelve, some of them moderately disturbed, who were awaiting placement in foster homes or institutions. It had recently been refurbished and divided into two sections. One-half continued to house young boys—about forty of them. About sixty teen-age girls, aged fourteen to eighteen, were housed in the other half. The girls were classified as "persons in need of supervision." Yet, quite obviously, many should have been receiving care in mental institutions and were classified as "disturbed."

Within six months of the girls' arrival, the shelter, the surrounding neighborhood, and the news media were in an uproar. Gangs had taken over in the girls' half; homosexuality, liquor, and drugs were rampant. Pimps, male gangs, and unsavory men had easy access to the shelter; one girl was lured into another girl's room and raped by a gang of youths. Two counselors were stabbed; another was stripped. Fires broke out frequently. While the girls were not imprisoned, they were supposed to obtain passes before leaving the shelter, and they had an 11:30 PM curfew. Neither the pass system nor the curfew was observed.

The counselors picketed, demanding more staff (they were about one-hundred below a full complement). They demanded that the most disturbed girls be removed. They complained that medical facilities at the shelter were inadequate.

Most of the girls were on tranquilizers, but, every time a counselor administered medication, he or she realized that the girl, made docile, would be at the mercy of other disturbed girls. A number of weaker and less antisocial girls told of being terrorized by the girl gangs. The younger boys on the other side were in terror, too. One retarded boy was nearly drowned when a group of girls held his head down in a toilet bowl.

Obviously, the children in the shelter were not receiving the type of care they needed. Yet, because of the bureaucracy, little could be done except to calm the situation on the surface through the installation of guards and stronger discipline. The bureaucracy was in large measure responsible for the situation in the first place. Overcrowded mental institutions often refused to accept youths who were referred to them by the juvenile court, The court, faced with the problem that the youths had not committed any criminal acts, were than forced to categorize them as persons in need of supervision and to send them to shelters for such "PINS," as they were called. The shelters did not have adequate facilities or staff to handle them and, once they were admitted, the youngsters often became even more disturbed and preyed upon those who were not.

This is only one case. Conditions are better in some institutions and as bad or worse in others. The reason for the recurrence of such horror stories is the chronic lack of interest shown by the public and its representatives in the fate of troubled youth.

Obviously, the prime remedy is to spend more money on more and better facilities; but until they are made available, there are few ways for individuals to escape present conditions.

The Standard Juvenile Court Act provides a way:

A parent, guardian, or next friend of a minor whose legal custody has been transferred by the court to an institution, agency, or person may petition the court for a modification or revocation of the decree, on the ground that such legal custodian has wrongfully denied application for the release of the minor or has failed to act upon it within a reasonable time, and has acted in an arbitrary manner not consistent with the welfare of the child or the public interest.

In order to take advantage of this provision, however, a youth needs some adult to care about him or her enough to petition the court to this effect. Such an adult is not always available. It is highly unlikely, for example, that the youths in the children's shelter described earlier had such caring adults to act for them.

Either new laws must be instituted to allow youth who have no caring adults to act for them to act for themselves in petitioning the court to remove them from places of detention where conditions are intolerable, or the public must show greater interest in the institutions to which they send troubled youth. While at the outset this might seem nearly impossible, there is the possibility that the movement for prisoners' rights that began in the early 1970s will pave the way for more concern with the rights of young people in detention facilities. In the late summer of 1974, a made-for-television movie, *Born Innocent*, treated the subject of conditions in juvenile detention homes, and there is no better place to take a case for reform than to the living room TV.

There is no question that juvenile justice is the area in which there is the most to be done to secure youth rights, and yet it is also the area in which the problems are most complex. The condition of the juvenile justice system is in large measure a symptom of conditions in the larger society. Until we get rid of poverty and discrimination and all of the other ills of our society that breed young offenders, even the most efficient and well-equipped juvenile justice system will not be able to handle all of the youths placed in its charge.

Until we rid ourselves of these basic ills, the best that can be done is to provide that a great deal more money be spent on better institutions and better treatment for those in need of medical care. Such money might be forthcoming if enough people, including young people not in trouble with the law, pressured for it.

5
Youth and Rights at Home

UNTIL ABOUT THE middle of the nineteenth century, children were regarded basically as the possessions of their parents. Parents' control over their children was unquestionable. A father who beat his child or a mother who forced her child to work long hours might have been disapproved of by the community, but no one in the community would have seriously questioned their right as parents to treat their children in whatever way they wished. The community might have felt sorry for the child, but no one would have suggested that the child had an actual legal right to proper treatment.

In the last half of the nineteenth century, this situation began to change, and since then the rights of children in relation to the rights of parents have slowly but steadily enlarged. We have already discussed this change in the areas of school and labor. In both cases, the state intervened and took away parental control. Despite what the parents wanted, the state decided that all children between certain ages should go to school and that all children between certain ages should be protected against excessive labor.

Another area in which youth rights began to be recognized in the last half of the nineteenth century was that of physical punishment. Taking rights away from parents in this area was a very difficult problem, because one of the best recognized and most widely exercised rights of adults was physical punishment of youth. And when the children were away from their parents, in school for example, it was felt that teachers and other school personnel had the same right, for they were acting *in loco parentis*, or in the place of parents. Yet, in the last half of the nineteenth century a distinction began to be made between "punishment" and "abuse." Here, too, the state of Illinois showed itself a leader in the area of youth rights, in the case of *Fletcher et al.* v. *Illinois* in 1869.

Samuel Fletcher, Jr., who was blind, was imprisoned by Samuel Fletcher, Sr., his father, and Ledicia Fletcher, his stepmother, in a cold and damp cellar during several days in mid-winter. Somehow, the boy escaped, and the town authorities brought suit against his parents. At the trial, the only excuse the father could offer was that the boy was covered with vermin. He could not explain why his son, blind and helpless, had come to be in such a state in the first place.

The court found Samuel Fletcher, Sr., and Ledicia Fletcher guilty and sentenced them to pay a fine of $300 each (no small sum in 1869!). While admitting that the law gave parents broad authority over their children, the court stated, "It would be monstrous to hold that under the pretense of sustaining parental authority, children must be left, without the protection of the law, at the mercy of depraved men or women, with liberty to inflict any species of barbarity short of the actual taking of life."

The *Fletcher* case was an individual case, and it was through such individual cases that the right of youth to be protected from physical abuse by their parents first began to be recognized. The first organized effort for the protection of children did not take place until five years after the *Fletcher* case.

In 1874, the New York Society for the Prevention of Cruelty to Children (SPCC) was founded. The SPCC was an outgrowth of humane work for animals such as the Society for the Prevention of Cruelty to Animals (SPCA), which says something about American values! At any rate, the New York SPCC was copied widely, and by 1900 over 250 such societies were in existence throughout the country.

Originally, most of these societies had broad enforcement powers. Agents of the New York SPCC, for example, wore police badges and were empowered to act as officers of the law. They were thus able to enter a home where child abuse was suspected and, if they found evidence of abuse, to arrest the adult or adults involved and to remove the child to an institution for children. After the turn of the century, however, the number of children in institutions because they had been abused at home, combined with the number of youths committed to institutions by the new juvenile courts, had become a brand new problem. The trend now was toward reform and rehabilitation of the parents, in order that a youth who had been abused could remain at home. The anticruelty societies reduced their law-enforcement tactics and concentrated upon family counseling.

There were humane reasons, as well as practical reasons (overcrowding), for this change. The prevailing attitude in our society has always been that, except in extreme cases, children are better off at home with their natural parents, and generally this is the right attitude. Without it, there would be many cases where a child would be removed from a basically loving and supportive home because of one rash act by a parent. Such a case occurred in Louisiana in 1947.

A mother visited her doctor's office and took her infant with her. The baby cried, and both the doctor and his nurse warned the mother that the crying was disturbing the other patients. The mother was placed in a room by herself, where she apparently spanked the child. The police were called and the baby was taken from his mother.

At the trial, a doctor testified that the baby was physically normal, had a comfortable home, and good care. Another doctor testified that the mother was mentally capable of taking care of her baby. Yet, the court declared the child to be neglected and ordered it placed in an orphan asylum.

The mother took her case to the Louisiana Supreme Court, which reversed the lower court's decision. The mother had obviously been very embarrassed, even agitated, about her baby's crying in the doctor's office. While it was wrong for her to spank the baby, it was quite certain that she normally took good care of him. The

Supreme Court recognized that the spanking was not enough to justify taking the baby from her.

Still, the attitude that a child should remain at home except in extreme cases holds great dangers for children. Never was this more evident than in the case of Roxanne Felumers. An abused child, Roxanne had been taken from her mother and stepfather and placed in a foster home. The mother, however, missed the child and went to a variety of voluntary social agencies for help. One of these voluntary agencies recommended that the New York City Family Court remove Roxanne from her foster home and return her to her mother and stepfather, and in 1969 the Family Court did so. Shortly after, her stepfather killed her.

In the public outcry and investigation that followed, shocked judges and social agencies referred every child to a shelter whenever there was the slightest suspicion of abuse. The population of the shelters swelled to bursting; and, given the state of many of the shelters, as described in the previous chapter, this was no solution to the problem of the children's rights either.

Today, the law, while definite in establishing a child's right to protection from abuse, is not very definite about what constitutes abuse. This is how the law reads:

> Either parent has the right and duty to inflict reasonable and moderate chastisement on the child for the punishment of faults or disobedience and the enforcement of parental authority, as long as he or she does it for the welfare of the child. A parent, however, has not the right in correcting a child to inflict punishment which is excessive, immoderate and unreason-

able, under the circumstances, and, if this right to chastise is abused the parent is amenable to the criminal law, and the courts may punish the parent in a criminal proceeding for gross abuse of power over the child resulting in an injury. The authority of a parent to chastise the child may be delegated to another.

The words *excessive, immoderate,* and *unreasonable,* are as vague when used to describe physical punishment as the word *extreme* is vague in school hair and dress regulations. They give adults an awful lot of leeway in the punishment they can administer and give the courts great leeway in deciding what is reasonable punishment and what is abuse. How the courts choose to interpret the law depends greatly upon societal attitudes and the times. From about 1900 to 1969, the attitude was that the child should remain at home except in extreme cases. In 1969 an extreme case occurred, and the attitude changed; in fact, it nearly reversed. The current feeling is that the child has the right to be removed from an abusive home.

A problem, however, is that sometimes this right conflicts with another right—the right of children to live where it is in their best interest to live. Sometimes, an abused child is better off at home than in a shelter where drugs, homosexuality, and violence are rampant. But it is questionable whether either alternative is in the child's best interest. Declaring this right is like saying that everyone old enough to work has a right to a job when there are clearly not enough jobs to go around. What good is a right when it is impossible to exercise it?

The problem of child abuse does not affect those of you

who are reading this book as much as it affects younger children, although it could have affected you greatly when you were younger. The younger the child, the greater the problem—for obvious reasons. The problem is most acute for children under age five. Of children in this age group, more die as victims of child abuse than from all childhood diseases combined. In the first place, most children under five are not old enough and do not have enough experience to know that they are being abused. They may know they hurt, but they do not know that children as a rule are not hurt as they are. Also, children under five are usually unable to express themselves enough to tell anyone else what happens to them. They can say, "My mama hit me" or "My daddy made me stay downstairs." They may not know how to express that they are beaten severely or locked in the cellar for several days. Then, too, the majority of children under age five do not go to school, where a teacher might discover evidence of abuse.

The older the child, the more likely that abuse will be brought to the attention of the authorities in some way. The trouble is, it is up to the authorities or some family agency or some concerned adult to bring charges against the abuser or abusers. Whether you are seven or seventeen, you do not have the right to bring these charges yourself. Someone else has to do it for you.

Some states do have statutes that permit minors to sue their parents in civil court for injuries received from corporal punishment; but the courts are not in full agreement about this right. If you feel you have been abused, you should ask an adult whom you feel cares about you—a relative, a teacher, a school counselor—about the possibility of bringing charges.

There is some hope that youth will, in the future, be granted greater rights in the area of protection from abuse. Experts calculate that 50,000 young people die from it every year, and there is no calculating how many are seriously injured. The problem is being exposed in its full dimensions in newspapers and magazines and on television, and it is likely that eventually the courts will be forced to respond with some protective laws.

In the meantime, however, American society will have to make a greater effort to provide healthy alternative homes and institutions for abused youth. Otherwise, one problem will merely be exchanged for another.

Another area in which youth rights have been recognized is that of higher education. A century ago, parents were not obligated to provide their children with any schooling at all; by the 1970s some courts were deciding that parents were obligated to put their minor children through college, if they could afford to do so. This is how the law looks at the question:

> In determining what education is necessary for a particular child, consideration must be given to the progress of society and the attendant requirements on the citizen of today. And it has been pointed out that a college education was a rarity at the time of these early decisions (wherein the court denied that this was a parent's obligation), but under modern conditions may be as necessary, especially for some callings, as an

elementary or high school education formerly was. And the fact that the state maintains institutions of higher learning supported by public funds has been taken as indicating a public policy that a college education should be available to all. Accordingly, the trend of recent authority is to the effect that under modern conditions and in proper cases, education beyond that provided in common schools may be a necessary which a parent is obliged to provide for his child, and that a parent able to do so may be required to bear the expense of a college education for a child evincing an aptitude therefor. Determination as to whether a parent should be so required in a particular case will depend on such factors as the financial condition of the parent, the statutory age of majority, whether the child is self-sustaining, and whether the parent has agreed to provide such education. A decree requiring a parent to pay for a college education for his child will not be entered where this will impose an undue hardship on the parent . . . .

Thus, the law says that—if your parents can afford to put you through college, have previously agreed to do so, and then change their minds—in general, you have the right to insist they provide for your education. In some regions, however, you do not have this right and parents are relieved of the obligation to provide you with a higher education even if they are millionaires and you are a genius who wants to be doctor. And if your parents cannot afford a college education for you, or if college has never been discussed and suddenly, in your last year of high school you decide you want to go and your parents refuse, the law says they are not obligated to pay your way through college.

At first glance, the law may seem very liberal in regard to parental obligations to provide higher education, but remember that the law applies only to minors, and as more and more states are lowering the age at which a minor becomes an adult to eighteen, particularly now that eighteen-year-olds can vote, the law is being quite effectively rendered useless. The majority of entering college freshmen either are eighteen or will be before the end of their freshman year. As soon as they are eighteen they are on their own, and their parents have no legal obligation to them whatsoever.

At the end of the chapter "Youth and Labor," it was mentioned that minors do not have control over the money they earn. In most states, this is true even for those who do not live at home, although under some statutes the parents cannot get the child's earnings if they do not first notify their child's employer that they want them. The only state that gives parents no control over the money minors earn through their own labor is Louisiana.

The reason parents are generally given this control is connected with parents' obligation to financially support their children until they reach adult status and with childrens' obligation, in turn, to serve their parents until adulthood is achieved. The law not only involves wages but also extends to property—clothes, toys, gifts to the minor, etc.

Many people who are concerned with the rights of minors are urging that a distinction be made among the various kinds of property a minor can have, a distinction that would allow parents to retain control over some types but put others in the control of minors.

Money earned by the minor's own labor is one of the things that would be placed basically in the control of the minor, provided that it was handled wisely and fairly. If a parent lost his or her job and a son, who was earning $50 a week working part-time, refused to contribute any of his wages to help the family, then the parents should have some claim to at least part of his wages. If a girl wanted to use money she had earned to buy an electric saw with which to make furniture and her family lived in an apartment with thin walls, the parents ought to be able to forbid her to buy the saw.

Parents would be given control over things that would directly affect them. For instance, the sound of the girl's saw would bring complaints from the neighbors and possible threats of eviction. As it would be up to her parents to find and pay rent on another apartment if they were forced out of the first, they should be able to forbid the buying of the saw. Furniture and clothes that parents have bought for their children also fall into this category. Within the family, each child's furniture and clothing should be his or hers. He or she, however, should not have the right to sell or give away this clothing or furniture if the parents would then have to spend their money to replace the items.

Connected with the idea of control of money and ownership of property by minors is the question of a minor's right to make a will that is seen as binding by the courts. At present, you do not have this legal right until you are eighteen or twenty-one, in most states, although in Georgia and Puerto Rico you only have to be fourteen, and if you are a girl living in South Carolina you only have to be twelve.

In all states, however, you *should* be able to make a will that is legally binding, no matter what your age, subject to some conditions. You should not be able to leave all the furniture in your room, even if you have your own room, to your best friend if it means your parents will have to buy new furniture in order that a younger sister or brother might occupy the room.

But just as you should have some right to control money you have earned and personal gifts that have been given to you, so, too, you should have the right to will them to whomever you want.

In the majority of cases, young people probably do have these conditional controls over money and property. If you feel you do not, however, it is important that you find out what the law says in your particular state before taking any action. Then, if you find you do have a case, in most states you will have to get an interested adult to bring charges for you. You might or might not win your case, but if you did, it would establish a very important precedent and would help a lot of other young people win similar cases in the future.

To conclude, the status of the parent-child relationship is a changing one. Since the last half of the nineteenth century, the scale weighing the rights of parent versus child, which had been heavily weighted in favor of the parent, has been tipped slightly more in favor of the child. You are still not even with your parents, and, while a few more weights ought to be added to your side, it is probably not advisable for perfect balance ever to be achieved. In seeking your rights, you do not want to give up all your protections. The majority of parents do have their children's best interest in mind.

6
Youth and the Right to Choose a Home

THE MOST STRIKING thing about legal decisions regarding where or with whom children live is the lack of reference to the feelings of the *children themselves* in many cases. This is not to say that the children's feelings have not been taken into consideration in many of these cases, but it is a fact that they have not been given as much weight as they should have been; otherwise, they would have been mentioned in the written descriptions of the cases or the written decisions in the courts made upon them. Not giving the child the greatest say in the majority of cases involving where and with whom he or she will live is one of the most serious denials of youth rights in our history and in our society today.

Regarding the question where and with whom children will live, the law has traditionally held, and continues to hold, that children are best off living with their parents. In the case of divorce or other separation of parents, the general view is that children should live with the mother.

Just as there is nothing more sacred in our society than the relationship between mother and child, so there is nothing more sacred in the eyes of a child under the age of ten or so than his or her mother. This is true especially among the poor and among minority groups. Anyone who has lived in an urban, minority area, for example, knows that the greatest number of fights among young residents begin because one insults or even mentions the other's mother. One reason for this extreme mother loyalty is that often among poor people and minority people the father is absent, either because he is working away from home or because he has abandoned the family. Frequent father absence, due to work or divorce, is prevalent among middle- and upper-income families, too. The point is, the bond between mother and child is a very strong one, as has been traditionally recognized by the courts.

The idea that a child needs a natural mother or a substitute mother is so strong, in fact, that it has often taken precedence over the right of a natural or substitute father, *despite* the best interests of the child. The views that (1) living with the natural parents is best for the child; and (2) living with the natural mother or substitute mother or parents is better than living with the natural father or substitute father are probably correct in the majority of cases. There are exceptions, however, and the road to youth rights in this area has been a very uneven one, although it is possible to see a slight trend, in this era of recognition of children's rights, toward acknowledging what the child wants.

From colonial times up to about the middle of the nineteenth century, control of natural parents over their children's lives was generally unquestioned. Fathers could indenture their sons to craftsmen; poverty-stricken parents could essentially sell their children to work for others. Children who were abused at home and had run away to live with others would be caught and returned to their natural parents. There were no formal adoption laws. Children were adopted and disadopted in quite an informal manner, and always, the natural parents, if living, had the edge in deciding what would happen to the child. The child, legally, had no say in the matter whatsoever.

Formal recognition that the child has some right of choice occurred in the second half of the nineteenth century, when the first state laws regulating and formalizing adoption were passed. During this time, most northern and western states passed such laws. In the South, and in Iowa and Pennsylvania, adoption by deed continued, which meant that no formal agreement was signed and that, if a child lived with a person or persons other than its parents, then, in effect, it had been adopted.

Still, these early adoption laws left much to be desired, as did the procedures for screening adoptive parents. During the first quarter of this century, private adoptions were numerous, and the chief means of getting adopted children and adoptive parents together was, incredibly, newspaper advertising!

These are some of the ads that appeared in the *Chicago Tribune* between 1919 and 1921:

Personal—Wanted to Adopt Baby girl up to 4 years.

Will furnish ideal home and best refs. Address M476, Tribune. (December 4, 1921)

Personal—Wanted—Healthy Twins or Baby girl under 6 months, by couple able to give children wonderful home & future. Address KH 385, Tribune. (December 21, 1919)

Personal—Wanted for adoption by wealthy Chicago couple, infant girl or boy. Address KH 386, Tribune. (December 21, 1919)

Personal—Wanted to Adopt Baby month old, by responsible couple; good home. Address B 599, Tribune. (December 21, 1919)

Personal—Want Home. 7 Year old boy, adoption. Call 2932 Indiana Av., Chicago. (December 28, 1919)

In 1925, a commission appointed to study the statutes of Pennsylvania relating to children reported:

It was impossible to get any accurate idea of the amount of advertising carried on throughout the State both of babies for adoption and of requests for children. A survey made of the Pittsburgh newspapers which specialize in "wantads" showed that during a six months period twenty-five babies were advertised for adoption while in ten cases prospective foster parents were advertising for babies. . . . It would seem that an enactment making it illegal either to secure or to dispose of a baby through the medium of the newspapers would be in line with common sense measures of child protection.

The commission also studied actual conditions of adoptive homes and found many cases of neglect. In its final report, it recommended:

It is evident that adoptions which expose young children to neglect and hardship and an adverse and unsuitable home life do actually and will continue to take place if the adoption process continues to be unattended by the exercise of judgment and discretion on the part of those in authority to decree adoptions and if adoption by deed continues to be legally authorized. Without certain legally prescribed measures safeguarding the child's welfare, the exercise of discretion on the part of the individual judges and other officials is and will be of an uncertain nature.

Since 1925, of course, both advertisement for adoption and adoption by deed have been outlawed. This does not mean that all adoptions are carried out legally, though. Across the country, there exist underground adoption agencies, and even kidnapping rings, run for the sole purpose of providing childless parents with children. The majority of adoptions, however, are handled either through authorized adoption agencies or privately but with proper legal procedures.

The system is still flawed. As some widely publicized cases in the early 1970s showed, adoptive parents cannot always be sure the child they have adopted will be allowed to remain theirs. When there is a natural mother involved and she changes her mind and wants her baby back, quite frequently the courts will rule in her favor.

One of the most famous of these cases, the "Baby Lenore" case, occurred in New York in 1971. Olga Scarpetta, an unwed mother, surrendered her child to the Spence-Chapin adoption agency when the baby was two weeks old. Two weeks later, the baby was placed with the DiMartino family for adoption. Five days later, the mother decided she wanted to keep her baby after all and requested her return. The agency refused, and the mother instituted court action.

The trial court ordered the agency to return Lenore to her natural mother. The agency took the case to an appellate court and then to the New York Court of Appeals. Neither court would reverse the decision of the lower court. Meanwhile, the DiMartinos had tried to intervene in the proceedings but had been denied standing in the case.

The New York courts in this case held to the view that a baby was best off with its natural mother, providing that there was no evidence that she was mentally or physically unfit to care for the child. There was no mention of the DiMartinos; they were not even considered in the case.

The DiMartinos refused to surrender Lenore and took her to Florida, out of the jurisdiction of New York State. In Florida, Ms. Scarpetta again brought court action for the return of her baby, and a full hearing was held; this time the DiMartinos were allowed to participate. The Florida court decided the baby should remain with the DiMartinos. The mother attempted to take her case to the U.S. Supreme Court, but the Court refused to hear the case. Matters of adoption are the responsibility of the individual states; if the Supreme Court heard the case, it would take this responsibility away. Thus, as along as the DiMartinos remained in Florida, Lenore would remain theirs.

The "Baby Lenore" case brings to light many of the problems that still exist in the adoption processes in the United States.

First, there is the question of whether or not a natural mother should be allowed to reclaim her child after she has put him or her up for adoption. There have been cases, of course, in which it was proved that the mother was pressured into putting her baby up for adoption. In such cases, there is reason for considering her request to reclaim her child. In cases where the mother was not pressured and gave up her child willingly, then changed her mind *after* the child had been placed in a new home, what should be the courts' decision?

Second, there seems to be a great need for more uniform state laws on adoption. While this uniformity might endanger the individual states' rights to make their own adoption laws, it might also prevent the kind of flight to another state with different laws that the DiMartinos undertook.

Most important, there is the question of what effect publicity and a tug-of-war situation has upon the child. While Lenore was much too young at the time to decide with whom she would be better off living, when she grew older she would know about the fight between her adoptive parents and her natural mother. Other people would know about it, too.

The question of the child's own desires in adoption cases did not, as we have just mentioned, enter into the "Baby Lenore" case. However, it was recognized fairly early in the history of adoption laws in the United States that a child, at least of a certain age, had a say in the matter. The 1873 New York law is typical. Among its provisions is this: "The consent of a child, if over the age of twelve years, is necessary to its adoption." Although it is questionable that children should not have a choice in the matter if they are under age twelve, there are sound reasons behind such provisions for considerably younger children. Up to age six or seven, a child really has not the experience to decide with whom he or she wants to live. The natural mother or mother substitute has been the chief person in his or her life and, as was mentioned in the previous chapter, a child will cling even to a highly abusive mother, not having experienced any other mothering with which to compare hers. Even an older child who has been able to compare will often choose the natural mother.

The older a child gets, the more chances he or she has to come into contact with other adults, and it is a natural part of growing up to look to adults outside the family for affection, concern, and interest. Usually by the age of nine a child is able to make a realistic comparison between two adults or two sets of adults.

One last point should be made about adoption—particularly of children who were adopted at a very young age, too small to remember their parents or their parents' names. Present laws hold that adoption records are confidential and may not be opened even to an adopted child. Thus, an adopted child has no legal means to find out who his or her natural parents were.

There are good reasons for the confidentiality of these records. They could possibly be used for blackmail, extortion, and a host of other improper purposes. But to deny access to these records even to the adopted child is to deny the child the basic right to know who he or she is. A young person's desire to know about his or her real parents is natural. It does not mean he or she does not love the adoptive parents. It does not mean he or she wants to return to the natural parents. It is simply a desire to *know*. And denying the right to know usually causes many more problems and much more sorrow than granting it. No matter how much publicity and stigma "Baby Lenore" suffers when she grows up, she will be envied by many adopted youths. At least *she* will know.

Thus far in this chapter, we have been concerned with the matter of adoption. In cases where the question is legal custody of a child, the laws and customs do not differ greatly from those concerning adoption. Here, too, it is the responsibility of the courts to decide what is best for the child until about age twelve, although there are exceptions.

One of the cases on record in which the wishes of a child are mentioned in the written record concerned a nine-year-old girl in Florida. The parents of the girl, Dawn, were divorced in 1961, when she was four years old, and custody was awarded to the mother. The father filed a petition in juvenile court five years later in 1966 and won custody of his daughter, based on the argument that the mother was too poor to take care of their daughter properly. Dawn, through her mother, appealed the decision.

Cases involving where and with whom children will live are decided on an individual basis, and there are few precedents upon which these decisions are based. As a general rule, when the decision is between natural mother and natural father, in a divorce case, for example, and the children are under twelve, their custody is usually given to the mother. Children twelve or above usually have some choice in the matter. Also as a general rule, when the decision is between natural mother and one or more nonrelatives, the natural mother is favored. There are some cases, however, where this general rule has not held true.

The case of Jack Bayne does not actually involve custody. It does, however, involve the right of a person to decide who his parents are. Jack Bayne had no father, and his mother was very poor. When Jack was thirteen, he moved in with the Whitleys, a couple who were neighbors. He lived with the Whitleys for six years, until he graduated from high school and enlisted in the armed service. Meanwhile, he saw his mother often and had a warm relationship with her.

While in the service, Jack Bayne wrote warm, loving letters to both the Whitleys and his mother, although, when he returned home on furlough, he returned to the home of the Whitleys. After Jack Bayne died in service, it was discovered that he had left his national life insurance to the Whitleys. The mother contested.

In the trial that followed, the court examined the letters

received by both the Whitleys and the mother and found that while the young man's letters to his mother were warm and affectionate, it was clear in his letters to the Whitleys that it was to their home that he intended to return once he had been discharged from the service. The insurance he left was awarded to the Whitleys.

This finding, of course, was that of one individual court; it established no precedent for other court decisions. There, too, it dealt only with the matter of a young man's right to recognize the couple with whom he had lived as his substitute parents. Had his mother not given her permission for him to live with the Whitleys, he would have been unable to stay with them, and had he left his insurance to them, as neighbors, his wishes would probably have been overruled in court.

What about cases in which no natural mother is involved? What happens when the only natural parent living or around is the father? While in recent years there has been a trend toward recognizing that a father can be a fit parent, even without a wife, the courts are still very skeptical of fathers. While a natural mother is favored except in extreme cases, a natural father is not. He is somehow seen as being unable to provide a stable home life. The idea of a father and his son living free from day to day, without any structure, all the while trying to avoid the prying and suspicious eyes of social agencies, is a familiar theme in books and movies. Court disapproval of a father who is considered irresponsible continues, even if the father has remarried. This was true in the case of *Painter* v. *Bannister*.

Mark Painter, age five, was placed by his father in the

temporary care of his grandparents on his mother's side, the Bannisters, after the child's mother and younger sister were killed in a car accident. Two years later, Painter remarried, settled into a new home, and tried to get his son back. The grandparents refused to give Mark up, saying that the boy was better off on their Iowa farm than in San Francisco with his father.

Painter took the case to court and was awarded custody of his son. The grandparents appealed and the Iowa Supreme Court reversed the decision, returning Mark to the custody of his grandparents. The court's reasoning was typical of the general attitude toward natural fathers who lead a so-called Bohemian life, even if they have remarried.

The court said it was not questioning the father's fitness to raise his son, although it did rely on the testimony of a child psychologist that Mark might "go bad" if he moved from a stable environment to "an uncertain future in his father's home." What it did decide was this:

> The Bannister home provides Mark with a stable, dependable, conventional, middle-class middlewest background and an opportunity for a college education and profession, if he desires it. It provides a solid foundation and secure atmosphere. In the Painter home, Mark would have more freedom of conduct and thought with an opportunity to develop his individual talents. It would be more exciting and challenging in many respects, but romantic, impractical and unstable.
>
> . . . We believe . . . (life in the Painter household) would be unstable, unconventional, arty, Bohemian, and probably intellectually stimulating.

> . . . We believe security and stability in the home are more important than intellectual stimulation in the proper development of a child.

This decision was rendered in 1966, and it says a lot about the values of the Iowa Supreme Court. Probably, it also says a lot about the values and attitudes of our society in general. Stability, conventionality, mediocrity apparently are valued more highly than intellectualism, curiosity, stimulation. Perhaps that is why so many public school students become bored with school. Why does our society see averageness as the right of youth and uniqueness as a threat to youth?

It is good to know that ultimately, without any court case at all, Mark was returned voluntarily to the custody of his father.

Currently, there is much talk of and much agitation for women's rights, and this is as it should be. But there are areas where rights are also denied to men, and one area in which this is particularly true is that of child custody.

A natural father, however, has a greater opportunity to gain custody of a child than does an unmarried, non-relative, no matter how much he or she cares about the child. Traditionally, the right to adopt a child has been denied to single people, although in the 1970s a few single adoptive parents have been successful. In these cases, however, the natural parents were either deceased or had voluntarily given up the child for adoption. In cases where the natural parent, even if he or she neglects or abuses the child, is not willing to give up custody, there is little chance that a single non-relative will be able to gain custody. This is true even when the child in question is over age twelve. A situation in the state of Maine illustrates this point.

A woman who had been married several times, and had lived with several other men as well, had eight children. They were ill-clothed and ill-fed and frequently beaten, either by the mother or by one of her husbands or boyfriends. While the mother received money, either from the state or from her ex-husbands or from her boyfriends, she spent it on liquor rather than on her children. She insisted that she loved her children, but her drinking, her frequent absences, and her frequent moves with her family resulted in an extremely disoriented life for them.

During the time the family lived in a particular town, one of the woman's sons, a thirteen-year-old, became attached to the director of a drug-rehabilitation program in the town. (The boy was not in any way involved with drugs.) In turn, the director became attached to the boy and, through him, befriended the family, buying groceries and giving money to the mother for food and clothing for the children.

Meanwhile, the thirteen-year-old boy had begun to spend weekends with the man, who was not married, and, in time, with the tacit consent of the mother, he began to live with the man, who treated him as his son. With the man, the boy enjoyed balanced meals, new clothes for school, concern and interest, and visits to the man's own parents and brother and sister, who accepted the boy as one of the family. The boy responded well to this new environment and gained self-confidence; his grades in school improved. In the meantime, contact was continued with the mother through frequent visits. The subject of adoption or legal custody was broached by the man, but the mother would not hear of it.

Then, several months after the boy had begun living with the man, the mother changed her mind about the arrangement. Previously, she had asserted that the man's concern was the best thing that could have happened to her son; suddenly she charged that the man had taken her son from her. Two considerably older sons forcibly removed the boy from school one day and took him to another town, refusing to allow any contact between the man and the boy.

The man consulted a lawyer as well as appropriate state offices. He was told that he had no legal grounds to seek custody of the boy. He was also told that it would be nearly impossible to have the mother declared unfit. Several weeks later, the mother allowed the boy to return to the man. Several more weeks later, the boy was again forcibly removed from school and taken to another town. Back and forth he went, always at the instigation of his mother, who either threw him out of her home or had him forcibly removed from the school in the town where the man lived. The man could do nothing without risking a kidnapping charge.

His appeals to the appropriate state offices brought responses like "Mind your own business," "It is no concern of yours," and "No, we are not investigating the woman and have no intention of doing so." Meanwhile, the woman's oldest daughter attempted to help her younger brother. She filed a formal complaint against her mother, listing fifteen witnesses to the mother's unfitness. (One of the witnesses was a former boyfriend of the mother's, in jail at the time for attempting to rape one of her younger daughters.) When the man inquired as to whether the service would investigate the daughter's complaint, the response was, "She's as crazy as her mother."

Meanwhile, the boy had turned fifteen and had become very skilled at dealing with the situation. When his mother threw him out, he went directly to the man who had befriended him. He insisted that there always be an open window in the man's home, a window through which he could escape if there came a knock at the door. He became adept at going underground when he heard his mother or older brothers were in the area. But he was very nervous; he could not concentrate on his schoolwork; the early glimmer of self-confidence had subsided in the face of his constant fear of capture. The man had begun to put aside money for the boy's education at college or vocational school; but neither he nor the boy was sure it would ever be used for that purpose. They knew that the man had no chance of gaining custody of the boy. They knew the boy had no legal right to choose where and with whom he would live. All either could hope for was that the boy could somehow survive until he was legally old enough to live by his own choice.

It is easy to criticize, particularly in this case. Yet, the people in the social-service agencies of the state of Maine can hardly be singled out as the villains when it comes to denial of youth rights in regard to where and with whom to live. Most likely, they are caring people, but their actions and responses showed a tendency toward the safe route.

There are reasons behind not favoring an unmarried, unrelated man in a custody case. Homosexuality (or prostitution) is one. So is "Faginism," named after the character in *Oliver Twist* who got young boys to steal for him. Yet, it does not matter if no hint of homosexuality or prostitution or Faginism is present—automatically denying custody of a minor to an unwed, nonrelated man is safe. So, too, refusing to investigate charges against a natural mother is the safe route. Uninvestigated charges are unproved charges, and unless a child dies or is seriously injured physically in the home of a natural mother, few would question a child's being made to remain there.

But what about the youth? What about what is safe for the youth? Unfortunately, these questions have taken a back seat to the question of what is safe for those who work with youth. Only exposure of such denials of youth rights will lead to those rights being made a primary consideration.

Tragic as the cases above might seem, there are even more tragic situations among youth today—those who are in institutions such as reform schools and children's shelters, either because their parents do not want them or because they do not want to live with their parents, and who do not have anyone else to care for them. These young people are really in a bind. They have committed no real crimes; yet, under our present laws, they have no place to live. Thus, they are placed in institutions. These youth have no choice at all. They are unwanted at home; they are unhappy in institutions; and there are no caring adults willing to take them into their homes.

Some adults who are concerned with the rights of young people have suggested that youths who are in institutions simply because they are not wanted by or do not want to live with their parents should be given alternative choices. They should be allowed to find other guardians, or to live as independent citizens. Naturally, these people do not rule out the possibility that a young person might choose neither alternative, and they recognize the need for institutions for such young people. The point is, of course, that if we lived in a society that allowed youth alternative choices, then our institutions would be much more humane as well.

These same people would also offer the same alternative choices to young people who were not confined to institutions, who did have parents or guardians. They would offer these young people the chance to live as independent citizens, for example.

Actually, the idea of full responsibility for minors is not new. It is possible for young people to be recognized legally as being on their own. They have to be over a certain minimum age, generally eighteen. They must be able to support themselves financially and indeed already be supporting themselves. Their parents must have given their consent for them to leave. If these conditions are satisfied, the young people are called emancipated. An emancipated young person is one who is free from his or her parents' control.

The main point here, in connection with youth rights, is that in almost every case emancipation can be granted solely by the parent. Only in a few cases, such as when a youth is abandoned or deserted by the parent or when a father who is able to support his child forces him or her to leave home and get a job, can minors be considered emancipated without parental consent.

The difference between the emancipation now recognized by law and the right to live independently mentioned earlier is that those who propose that youth be given the right to live independently would allow the young people to emancipate themselves. Also, they would lower the age at which youth could emancipate themselves to sixteen.

There are many young people who are currently on their own at age sixteen, even if they are not legally emancipated. There are many who would prefer being on their own legally to living at home under intolerable conditions. And if they could live independently, this does not mean they could not, later, either return to their parents or choose a secondary guardian.

The child and a secondary guardian would mutually agree to their relationship, either for a stated period of time or for an indefinite period. Or, the child might choose to live as an independent citizen for a certain period of time.

All the while, the primary guardians (the child's parents or, if the parents are dead, the child's appointed guardian) would remain primarily responsible for the support of the child and for the child's acts. While the child was living with a secondary guardian, this responsibility would be shared by both primary and secondary guardians. When and if the child left his or her secondary guardians, full responsibility would then return to the primary guardians.

In sum, the child would be given freedom of choice as to

where and with whom to live and could move from the primary-guardian relationship to the secondary-guardian relationship to independence and back again if he or she desired. The point is to allow youth as much freedom of choice as adults enjoy, as great a chance at happiness as possible.

While this all might seem rather fanciful, actually it is often done already. Children live with grandparents, aunts and uncles, even nonrelated people who all serve, in effect, as secondary guardians.

One of the people who supports the idea of the secondary guardian is John Holt. In his book *Escape From Childhood* he cites a situation in his own youth where the secondary guardian idea would have been useful:

> During my early teens, like many other young people, I was not always on the very best of terms with my parents. A close friend of mine was in the same situation; when I went to his home, he always seemed to be in some sort of hot water. But his parents liked me, and my parents liked him. It would probably have been good for all of us if he could have lived for awhile with my family and I for awhile with his. In time the novelty would have worn off; his parents would have begun to see faults in me, and I in them, and the same with him and my family. The parents would have learned that their children's faults were not unique, and the same for the children. When we returned to our original relationships they would probably have gone more smoothly.

It is unlikely that such proposals will be accepted in our society in the near future, or ever. Yet, perhaps if proposals like this one were put before our society more often and received more publicity, greater consideration would be given to children's rights in the area of where and with whom to live. Presently all power is in the hands of the parent or legally appointed guardian; the right of children to choose their own guardians would perhaps put too much responsibility on children. It would seem, then, that due consideration, within the present legal framework, of the rights of the child in cases of adoption and custody would be a practical compromise, offering many more young people happier lives.

7
Securing Your Rights

Hopefully, this discussion of five areas of youth rights has helped you to understand something about where you, as a young American, stand today in relation to the rest of society, and how you got there. As we have shown, changes in youth rights quite frequently have been due not to agitation by young people themselves but to economic conditions (the compulsory education movement), attitudes of adults (the movement toward formalizing adoption procedures), and attitudes of society about all people, not just adults (for example, the anti-child-labor movement as part of the general movement against cruel labor conditions). This was almost always true until about the middle 1950s.

Since the civil rights movement, young people themselves have taken a much greater role in the fight for youth rights.

It was they who brought about many of the rights and freedoms students now enjoy at school. It was young people who gained for themselves the rights to due process.

There is no question that American youths today enjoy considerable power as a group, both in terms of their buying power and in terms of their voting power, although this latter power will be more potential than real unless more eighteen-year-olds exercise their right to vote and unless more young people below age eighteen make their wishes clear to those who can vote. Yet, as we have tried to show in this book, there are still many ways in which youths are treated as second-class citizens.

You may enjoy school. You may be perfectly happy with your parents. You may be allowed to keep and spend at will whatever money you earn. You may have your parents' assurance that, should you die young, the terms of your will, should you make one, would be respected. You may, in short, feel no particular need to fight for your rights. As we have shown, however, there are many youth in America today who do not enjoy one or more of the above components of the good life; and as long as even one young person is denied rights, then all young people's rights are in danger. As the adage says, "A chain is only as strong as its weakest link," and there are still weak links that need strengthening.

Selected Bibliography

Bremner, Robert H., ed. *Children and Youth in America: A Documentary History.* Vol. II: 1866–1932. Cambridge, Mass.: Harvard University Press, 1971.

Browne, Elizabeth W. *Child Neglect and Dependency: A Digest of Case Law.* Reno, Nevada: National Council of Juvenile Court Judges, 1973.

Cashman, Charles E. "Confidentiality of Juvenile Court Proceedings: A Review," *Juvenile Justice* 24 (1973): 30–40.

Cordasco, Francesco, ed. *Jacob Riis Revisited: Poverty and the Slum in Another Era.* Garden City, N.Y.: Doubleday & Company, Inc., 1968.

Gottlieb, David, ed. *Children's Liberation.* Englewood Cliffs, N.J.: Prentice-Hall, Inc., 1973.

Selected Bibliography

Gyory, Richard. *The Constitutional Rights of Public School Pupils.* New York: Fordham University Press, 1971; reprinted from *Fordham Law Review,* December 1971.

Handlin, Oscar, and Handlin, Mary F. *Facing Life: Youth and the Family in American History.* Boston: Little, Brown and Company, 1971.

Hine, Lewis H. "Children or Cotton?" *Survey* 31 (1914): 585-92.

Holt, John. *Escape from Childhood: The Needs and Rights of Children.* New York: E. P. Dutton & Co., Inc., 1974.

Lobenthal, Joseph S., Jr. *Growing Up Clean in America.* New York: The World Publishing Co., 1970.

Loeb, Robert H., Jr., in consultation with John P. Maloney, J.D. *Your Legal Rights as a Minor.* New York: Franklin Watts, Inc., 1974.

McHardy, Louis W. "An Assessment of Juvenile Probation Services," *Juvenile Justice* 24, (1973): 41-46.

Polow, Bertram. "Reducing Juvenile and Domestic Relations Caseloads," *Juvenile Justice* 24, (1973): 47-54.

Sloan, Irving J., J.D. *Youth and the Law: Rights, Privileges and Obligations.* Dobbs Ferry, N.Y.: Oceana Publications, Inc., 1970.

Spargo, John. *The Bitter Cry of the Children.* Chicago: Quadrangle Books, 1968; first published in 1906 by Macmillan Co., New York.

Index

Index

Index